Strength, Resilience, Growth

How I Defied Physical and Mental Limitations and Took
Control of My Future

Sophia Rose Gigante

For my younger self.

CONTENTS

ACKNOWLEDGMENTS

There are two people that deserve as much recognition as this book will ever receive. Those two people are my parents. I would like to acknowledge my mother and father, Carla and John Gigante.

Thank you, Mom and Dad for never giving up. For always believing that I have a purpose. For going above and beyond to make sure that all of my medical challenges do not take away my happiness.

Thank you for loving me unconditionally and supporting all of my goals. For pushing me to do my best in life, but also understanding that I am not perfect. For loving my imperfections.

Thank you for your strength, resilience, and growth. I love you both more than you will ever know.

INTRODUCTION

My name is Sophia Rose Gigante. Most know me as "SRG," the Health and Wellness Coach, the Personal Trainer, the Nutrition Specialist. I am 22 years old and currently own a health and wellness business, "SRG FITNESS- Strength, Resilience, Growth." Each day, I walk into my studio thinking about how much I love what I do. Thinking about what brought me to choose this path. Thinking about the many personal hardships I've had to overcome, and still continue to work against every day. I always have my dad's voice in the back of my head, "Every day, in every way, you're getting better and better," something he has said to me since I was born.

After spending years battling numerous medical conditions, such as Hydrocephalus, Hypotonia, Strabismus, and seizures, it was up to me to change my life for the better. Fitness has helped me take control of my body after not being able to for so many years. The second I experienced this intense motivation, I knew this was my calling. The moment I saw how I was able to turn my life around was when I realized I wanted to change lives. Even if I could only change one person's life and see that they could have a similar outcome as I had, I would be fulfilled. This was when I decided that personal training, nutrition, health, and wellness was for me. I first got a job at my local gym, and I fell in love with it. I fell in love with seeing people achieve their goals and doing things they never thought possible. This is the feeling I also had when I started working out for the first time.

As a trainer, I work with individuals of all ages, limitations, and challenges, and I can see how health and fitness helps them and gives them a sense of purpose. The thrill I get from feeling and seeing their accomplishments assures me that I am where I am supposed to be.

I have learned that I do not just want to be a trainer at a gym. I want to help people in all aspects of health and wellness, physical fitness, nutrition, anxiety, and everything that I have ever had to go through. This is what prompted me to start SRG FITNESS.

This is the first time I ever had the courage and confidence to talk about my story, and I hope my story inspires you. It has taken me years to feel my own sense of strength, resilience, and growth. To feel like I fit in. To be able to look at the words "Hydrocephalus," "Hypotonia," "Strabismus," and "seizure," with pride instead of denial. Up until now, I have never addressed my medical conditions that disabled me from achieving any physical or mental feats. This is the story of how I finally took control of my body and live to inspire others to do the same.

Before you read this book, I want you to think about a challenge. A personal challenge. Whether it be one that you've overcome or one that you're working through. Think about it, and know that if you believe in strength, resilience, and growth, anything is achievable.

Strength, Resilience, Growth

1 EARLY CHILDHOOD TRAUMA

The Very Beginning

For some, childhood consists of playful times, happy memories, and carefree days. I wish that was the case for me. My story begins quite differently. April 5, 1998. The day that would bring me into existence. The day that initially started out to be the best day of my parents' lives. John and Carla, my parents, and the strongest people I know were more than ready to embark on life as caregivers.

Most infants are adored and praised by loved ones and doctors when they are first born. Most parents get to bathe in bliss as they start a new exciting chapter in their lives. However, the first words I had ever heard were unsettling. "At worst, she will grow up to be mentally disabled. At best, she will have severe learning disabilities. But she will definitely have physical ailments."

I was born with a brain condition called Hydrocephalus. My dad, being a medical professional, had only a little basic knowledge on what this meant. My mom had no idea. "hydro" refers to water and "cephalus" refers to the brain. But Hydrocephalus meant that I was going to have an incurable defect of my brain and spine. It disabled the natural flow of cerebrospinal fluid through my body, causing it to build up around my brain. If not caught in time, yes, I could have been mentally disabled.

Luckily, I was given the best possible care at NYU in New York City by, in my opinion, the most extraordinary neurosurgeon. There are not enough words in the world to describe Dr. Howard Weiner.

Imagine the stress my parents felt; they were new to having a child, and now they had to learn about an uncommon illness. Dr. Weiner was dealing with a newborn patient, along with confused, heartbroken, and anxious parents. He did so with complete ease. And made my first brain surgery, on April 28, 1998, extremely worthwhile. Since I was three weeks old, I have lived with a Ventriculoperitoneal Shunt, a bump on the back of my head, a big tube down my neck that I like to call a really sexy vein, and an unattractive scar on my stomach. All due to this surgery.

And that wasn't the end of it. From that moment on, I had gone through numerous checkups, uncomfortable MRIs, and just an all-around stressful first few months of life. As if the brain issues—that's what I refer to them when I don't like getting into detail with people—weren't enough, now I was about to face another challenge, Hypotonia.

***

During the months that followed my surgery, my parents noticed that I did not reach any of the physical milestones that I should have been reaching. I had some "features of gross motor delays." This is what started my journey with Hypotonia, or low muscle tone. It all stems back to my Hydrocephalus, but my low muscle tone has been something that has always left a mark on me. I was diagnosed with it shortly after my brain surgery and made aware that I had right-sided weakness. Now, to add on to the head bump, the tubing, and the ugly scar, I would have to wear foot braces and endure multiple physical therapy sessions for as long as I needed to correct this ailment.

Abba, one of my favorite bands from the 70s, has a song called "Thank You for the Music." The song explains how, despite life's challenges, as long as there is a song in your heart, anything is possible. There is so much truth to this in my early years of life. Although I couldn't walk, I had rhythm and determination. Most importantly, I had a song in my heart. For a little girl who couldn't walk and had traumatic events happen to her so early on, I was able to carry a tune at just three months old. Mom and Dad said I would sing the melody to the Barney theme song. They knew from that moment that if I had to go through physical problems, I would always have music to fall back on. And they were right. But we will get into that later.

It took me 18 months to take my first steps, which wouldn't have been possible without the physical therapy or wearing the clunky feet braces. As I transitioned from infant to toddler, the Hydrocephalus was now adding yet another problem to my childhood. Strabismus. In simpler terms, I not only had a lazy eye, but I couldn't see properly out of both my eyes. This caused unintentional injuries, and years of broken bones and frustrated bike rides as I could never fully see what was in front of me.

By 2 years old, I had a brain surgery, a physical disability, and one of two eye surgeries under my belt! Damn. There I was, head bump, tubing, ugly scar, feet braces, and now an eye patch. YIKES. Apparently, I took everything like a champ, at least for the first few years of life when I didn't really know what was going on. I'm sure I thought it was normal to look like a pirate and miss out on the playground for physical therapy sessions. No big deal. I wish I had always had that mentality. But again, at least I still had my voice.

Strength, Resilience, Growth

2   THE EARLY YEARS

Beginning Elementary School

For as long as I can remember, my style consisted of a blue plaid jumper or skirt, a white polo with my school's logo covering the left portion of my chest, and knee-high socks that were unbearably cold in the winter. This was Catholic grammar school. Ten years of it, to be exact. Growing up in suburban Westchester County, New York, going to Catholic school was almost inevitable. Although I hated the uniforms and the strict conduct, I understand now why my parents chose to put me in Catholic School. It was a safe haven for them to leave their sick kid.

My first few years of elementary school never seemed to be a problem for me. Sure, I would miss out on playdates and school functions due to numerous, unenjoyable, physical therapy appointments, doctor visits, and sometimes overly cautious parents, but this was all stuff I was used to.

Physical Therapy

Physical therapy was part of my weekly routine. Like kids would have scheduled baseball practices or dance lessons, I had three to four days a week of tortuous stretching and rehabilitation work for my Hypotonia.

My mom brought me to every single physical therapy appointment without missing a beat. She was a mother of a not-so-ordinary child, but worked hard to make sure I was progressing. She did so despite working a full-time job and not having any help besides that of my dad. She used to carry me up and down the flights of stairs in our apartment building because I was incapable of climbing them myself. But my mom knew that if she put her mind to it and did whatever it took to get me stronger, I would eventually be able to walk without any problems. My mom would take me outside and make me walk on the edge of the sidewalk to practice balance. She would make me walk backward instead of forward to work on coordination, along with many other techniques. She would spend all of 10 years taking me for monthly fittings for my foot braces. My mom would sit and hold me when I would cry about having to stick my feet into molding clay, instead of going on playdates with my friends. Despite everything I was going through, my mom was never afraid for me. She wanted me to be challenged. She wanted me to fall so I could practice getting myself back up. She believed I had strength, resilience, and growth, even when no one else did.

If there is one person I have to thank and apologize to, it's my therapist, Myrielle. Saying I acted like a whiny little bitch during my appointments is definitely an understatement. As someone who now preaches about the benefits of health and physical activity, I hated every minute of it back then. I would rather have been sitting at home eating my mom's English muffin pizzas with a side of Doritos or going to get a hot fudge sundae with my dad. Instead, I had to go through hours of excruciating physical activity. I mean, it was bad enough I had to walk around in braces all day.

One of the hardest things for my body to comprehend was walking heel to toe. I used to only be able to walk on my tippy toes. I would even unintentionally keep my right arm up because I was unable to control its movement. I often had to go to the physiatrist and get shots of botox in my calves to keep my heels on the ground. Myrielle worked hard to "get my foot down." She would constantly say things like "Stop walking on your tippy-toes," or "Keep your back straight," or "Relax your arms when you walk," or "Wear your braces at night or else all of this will go to waste." Damn, do I sound like that now that I am a physical trainer? I probably do, and I hope I do. Because if I could be anything like Myrielle, or help anyone the way she helped me, I know I am doing my job.

Throughout these torturous years of physical therapy, school gym class, and afterschool sports, outside social play was never really in the cards for me. I couldn't keep up with the other kids because of my imbalances and right-sided weakness. I couldn't play team sports because my Strabismus disabled my peripheral vision, and I had absolutely no strength.

The Worst Memories

As a child, I absolutely hated Halloween. I dreaded going trick-or-treating with friends. They would run up to all the houses in a matter of seconds, grab all the candy, and never look back at who might be lagging behind. I was the one always lagging behind. I couldn't run as fast, or basically not at all. The excitement was always too much for my mind to handle. I would get tired quickly, and while my friends begged to stay out all night, I was always ready to go home.

One of the worst memories I have growing up is learning how to ride a bike. It was the most frustrating experience for both my parents and me. I did not have the strength, balance, or coordination to keep myself on the bike, which would cause fear and stress for my parents, especially my dad. It was never a fun time, and since then, it has never been something I've had a desire to do. Due to my imbalances and Strabismus, I even broke my arm three times in two years because I just did not have control over my body.

Despite all of this, I still had my voice. I was still able to sing my heart out to songs that I would make up off the top of my head. The lyrics and melodies always seemed to match. "Look at My Shoes" was my own personal favorite! This was the one thing that came easily to me. It was the one thing that was going to be mine. Both my parents and I knew how important music was to me, especially growing up around a musical family. If you had asked my relatives about my love for music, they would have said, "Sophia is meant to be a star!" My dad is a drummer and an all-around amazing artist, so music was introduced to me even before I was born. I always liked to joke and say I got no talent from my mom because she does not have an ear for music. However, as my story goes on, I learned I have more gifts from her than I could have ever imagined.

Since the softball team, the basketball team, and any other sport my school had to offer wasn't for me, I took the opportunity to participate in the school plays. And guess what? I was always one of the lead roles! I had been told that I had one of the most powerful voices for a kid my age. The school plays became such a big part of my life. I would perform, my mom would help the parent association with the sets, and my dad would help with the music. Life was great.

As I got older and busier, I didn't need Myrielle as often, or at all. So, I began to face a new demon. If my parents and I thought that Hydrocephalus and Hypotonia were challenging to deal with, there was no way we were ready to face these next few years.

Strength, Resilience, Growth

3   THE UNCONTROLLABLE DEMON

My First Seizure

People often ask me what my biggest fear in life is. Or why am I so "obsessed" with the gym? Or why do I freak out when I feel something out of the ordinary with my body? My answer is quite simple, although my experiences as a young kid are complex.

Normal kids are afraid of the dark when falling asleep, or afraid of the monsters in the closet, or afraid that mom and dad won't hear them if they call for help. But 8-year-old SRG was never afraid. I knew I was always in control of what went on around me. Dad always told me to "be aware." As long as I was aware, I was in control. I was never afraid until the night I fell asleep, woke up unexpectedly, and was no longer in control.

This was the night of my first seizure. I could picture myself falling asleep that night. Probably after finishing a piece of cake, a brownie, or an ice-cream sandwich because God knows the last thing I cared about was if it were healthy or not. Everything felt normal. Mom and Dad were watching the Honeymooners in the living room. The light was shining through my bedroom since we live in a small apartment, and everything is in close quarters. I dozed off after a long day of school and play practice. Ready for a great night's sleep.

I could feel my eyes opening. I could see everything in my room, but I felt this uncontrollable sensation down the left side of my body. From my face to my feet, I felt tingling. And not the calm tingling you feel when you are relaxed. This was something different. This was scary.

I don't remember how I did it, but somehow I got myself out of bed and into the living room. I couldn't speak, but Dad knew something was wrong. This was the first of many times I had ever heard my dad panic. And his panic made my mom panic. I could hear him say, "SOPH! SOPH! What's wrong sweetie? Can you hear me? Say something?" But I couldn't. The tingling disabled me to respond. I was not in control.

My parents called 911 right away as my dad realized this was a seizure. Although this didn't last long in reality, it felt like a lifetime of events to me. I remember hearing sirens pull up outside of Gramatan Avenue. I was carried downstairs, into an ambulance where the paramedics quickly put oxygen around my mouth. "Sophia, are you OK, can you hear us?' But I couldn't respond. I was not in control. I was rushed to Lawrence Hospital in Bronxville, then transferred to Montefiore Hospital in the Bronx and given multiple tests and MRIs.

As it turned out, my first seizure was almost a blessing in disguise. As shocked as the seizure had left my parents and me, we were even more surprised to learn that the tubing of my VP shunt had been snapped, and it was time for another surgery. Ironically, the seizure was not due to the tube snapping. If I had not had the seizure at that time, my parents and I might have never known that anything was wrong with the shunt. So the big question is, did I ever grow out of the Hydrocephalus? Why didn't I have other symptoms after having a malfunction? Unlike my first brain surgery, I was now old enough to fully experience the fear that my parents had when I was three weeks old. I remember having to go under anesthesia before having my tube replaced, and my shunt re-evaluated. Honestly, I don't recall the sequence of events after this point. But any sense of normalcy I felt went out the window due to the new surgery and the seizures.

***

I don't remember all of my seizures in detail the way I remember my first. However, there are a few that stick out to me. I remember turning 9 years old and being at the American Girl Store in New York City. It was every little girl's dream to have a birthday party there. It was definitely my dream. When you live in New York, the American Girl Store is probably the closest thing to Disney World, except filled with dolls! I imagined it to be the best day as I walked inside with my mom, aunt, grandma, and a whole store of dolls around me. Everything was perfect until the seizures had to ruin it. I was standing in the middle of the store, surrounded by a flood of other little girls waiting to get their new doll. All of the chaos seemed exhilarating until my brain could not handle much more. All of a sudden, I became mute, just like that night in my bed. I could see and hear everything around me, but I was not in control. The tingling came back. Fear took me over, and before I knew it, I was back at NYU hospital. To this day, thirteen years later, I refuse to step foot near the American Girl Store. I have definitely been able to overcome some of my fears, but certain situations will always stick out.

After my second seizure, Mom, Dad, and I were told that it was not caused by another snap of the tubing, but it was the start of a seizure disorder. It was quite possible that I was going to grow out of it. But the road was long, the medications were endless, and the fears were unimaginable. So now, not only did I have neurosurgeon appointments, eye doctor checkups, and physical therapy, but I had to see a specialist for my seizures and frequent EEG testing. What a fun childhood.

Having Seizures in Elementary and Middle School

The night of my first seizure was the start of a very long disorder. Despite all of my other medical challenges, the seizures have left an unforgettable mark on me. Just hearing the word "seizure" or writing it out makes me feel extremely uncomfortable, anxious, and upset.

This disorder disabled me to be in control of my body. For years, I was in a constant waiting game. Waiting for the next seizure, and praying it would never happen at school. Luckily, it never did. Of all the seizures I ever had, I never had one at school. And boy, am I thankful. It was bad enough that I had to sit out of certain games during gym class or miss out on class trips. The last thing I needed was to get that horrifying, tingly feeling in front of all my friends.

During elementary and middle school, I had to miss class at certain points due to more surgeries, NYU doctor appointments, and important medical tests. I had to take my medication at the same time every night, and constantly check in with the doctor on my progress. I dreaded getting frequent EEG tests. Wires would be glued onto my head to test my brain waves, and I would be unable to move out of the hospital bed for days until the test was complete. It was torturous. It was uncomfortable. And it was unfair. I remember the only thing getting me through these tests was being able to watch Full House. This will forever be my favorite show. It brought me such joy during a terrible time. I was able to recite every line of each episode and would sing the show's theme song until my mom couldn't take it anymore! For a second, each time I would watch Full House, I would forget about what was going on in my reality.

For the majority of my childhood, I lived with never ending fear. I always felt when the seizure was coming, but I just never knew when to expect it. Whether they happened at home, in the car, during big events, or as I was falling asleep, the seizures were my uncontrollable demon.

Despite all these setbacks, I really did have an enjoyable time at school. I still had many friends as well as chorus, and the school plays to always look forward to. My parents had never made it a big deal that I had "issues." They showed strength, resilience, and growth throughout such a terrible time in our lives. They had no help. No one to bring me to the doctor if they needed time for themselves, and no one really to vent to about what they were going through. My parents supported each other, and they supported me.

None of my classmates ever knew the extent of anything going on in my personal life. If I had to sit out of an event, I would say, "I have some medical problems." But that was it. Mom and Dad kept this part of our lives pretty private because they never wanted me to feel different. They never wanted my challenges to define me. They wanted me to feel as normal as possible. Although I understand the reasoning and see how it has paid off, I wonder how I would have turned out if we were a bit more open. Would I have grown up to be as guarded as I am? Would it have taken me 22 years to open up about this? Would I have as much anxiety as I do? Would I have as much trouble cultivating close relationships?

***

By middle school, singing had become my greatest joy. Everyone knew me as the singer of the school. I would sing in the halls, go to every and any Broadway musical, participate in all of the music programs offered, and take the lead in the school plays. I loved to sing more than anything. I had such an ear for music that I could sit in front of a piano, listen to a song, and easily pick out every note. From *Mary Poppins* to *Bye Bye Birdie*, nothing was stopping me.

If you would have asked me what I wanted to be when I grew up, my answer was always "a Broadway star" or "a famous singer" or "a graduate from Julliard." Never in a million years would "a health and wellness professional," be my answer. I started voice lessons around the 7th grade. I always felt like a badass because I knew the technical terms of music before any other kid at school. There I was, now in my tweens, heavy on seizure medication, totally inactive, but working my way up to being a music professional.

Music was one of the only things that got me by during middle school. I would forget about my daily struggles whenever I sang a tune. I would forget about the numerous doctor appointments, the unbearably long EEG tests, and the MRIs that sometimes took hours to get the proper brain images. Alongside all of this, being on seizure medication made it extremely hard to focus, learn new material, and do well on tests. But it didn't matter. All I looked forward to was after school play practice, my big bag of Fritos, and a Reese's peanut butter cup just in case I was still hungry.

Besides music, there was another thing that would get me through my tedious years of school. This was the beach club. I spent almost every childhood summer at Beckwith Pointe Beach Club in New Rochelle. I was always surrounded by great friends, family, and lots of summer food! Most of my close friends growing up were those from the beach club. We did everything from swimming, kayaking, and basketball, to walking down the street for frozen yogurt. I always looked forward to being able to stay late on Friday and Saturday nights, watch the band perform, play manhunt, and go night swimming. This was the one place I actually felt like a real kid. It was the one place my parents felt comfortable enough to let me roam freely. I was able to feel safe and be active. I did not have to think about any of my medical concerns. Or at least that's how my parents made it seem.

I know now that the reason my parents chose to spend the summers at Beckwith was that it was safe for a child with unpredictable medical problems. All of the members of the club looked out for one another. The adults always made sure that the kids were safe while roaming around the grounds at night. And most importantly, I was always treated as an equal both physically and mentally by my peers. So, for the chance I had a seizure underwater, or if I fell because I couldn't judge my surroundings, I was in good hands.

For the most part, I have nothing but wonderful memories of the beach club. However, I will never forget the day I had a seizure there. It was on one of my friend's birthdays. Of course, another day that was supposed to be joyous. Surprisingly, unlike my American Girl Store experience, I was still able to enjoy my time there after this day. However, I remember each year after that having extreme anxiety on my friend's birthday. I think the reason I will never forget this arrival of the tingly feeling is because it happened at the one place I loved the most.

As one can imagine, as a young girl going through all the shit I was going through, I started experiencing a lot of anxiety. I always had trouble falling asleep at night or would freak out if I felt a slight tingle. I would start overthinking everything around me, and I even experienced a few panic attacks. I dreaded going to the dentist and used to make it a very unenjoyable experience for both my mom and me. Having Hydrocephalus and seizures meant that I had to be extra cautious when getting any type of dental work done. Before each appointment, I would have to take loads of medication that would make me sick to my stomach. I would scream, cry, and be extremely unreasonable during every dentist appointment, especially when getting braces.

Although all of the irritation and anxiety was unfair for a young girl, it was completely understandable. I became so angry inside. The things that used to make me laugh gave me absolutely no joy. I always felt as though I was walking on eggshells. I was waiting for something terrible to happen. I was waiting for the next seizure. I was so frustrated as to why this all had to happen to me. It was so unfair.

Strength, Resilience, Growth

Strength, Resilience, Growth

4   BECOMING A TEENAGER

Ending the Seizures

From 8 years old to 15, this seven-year block of my childhood was anything but easy. The seizures were traumatic, out-of-body experiences that, in my opinion, I did not deserve. I remember the long process of getting weaned off the seizure medication, once I stopped having them as often. Every couple of weeks, I would stop taking some of the pills and get monitored to see how my body reacted. This part of the journey took forever to complete, and it was anything but enjoyable. I would still have to go in for regular EEG tests to see if I had any abnormal brain wave activity. To get off the medication, I had to be seizure-free for two years. Then, I had to be seizure-free for another two years before I would be cleared completely.

One summer day in 2013, my mom, dad, and I went to my neurologist in New York City. It was beautiful outside. The sun was shining without a cloud in the sky. It was a perfect day. And it became even better when Dr. Lajoie told my parents and me that I would no longer be experiencing those tingly, uncomfortable, unpredictable episodes. My mom and dad both had tears running down their faces as my most recent EEG images were shown and explained to us. Just as predicted, I had ended puberty and grown out of this terrible disorder. It sure was something to celebrate. However, for some reason, I felt as though I didn't care. When reminiscing about this moment, all I can think of is my young teenage self, feeling almost "too cool" to shed a tear. Or not even feeling as though there were any tears to shed. I will never forget what I promised myself that day: "Sophia, the seizures are done, they are not a part of you, they do not define you. From now on, none of your medical problems exist. So you will never EVER acknowledge this experience." At the time, this seemed fitting for someone my age after going through all that I did. But would it really pay off in the long run?

I vaguely remember life without the seizures, and most of my "memories" are from what my parents tell me. Apparently, I was always filled with joy, always smiling, always singing with a Janis Joplin edge. I never let the Hydrocephalus, the Hypotonia, the numerous eye surgeries, or doctor's appointments bring me down. But as happy as I was to be done with the seizures, I was never as happy as that little girl.

***

Becoming a teenager is a hard transition in life for anyone. But transitioning into a new life stage after undergoing such a horrible time made it even tougher for me. My anxiety issues—that I still deal with today—started to really kick in. Alongside all of the intense emotions, being on a heavy dose of medication for years caused many unwanted, unattractive, and uncontrollable side effects. Believe it or not, SRG of SRG FITNESS was not always so fit. In fact, I was quite the opposite.

While being weaned off of the medication, my body did not always react well. The medication caused me to overeat and gain weight. It also caused extreme fatigue, which made any type of physical activity seem dreadful. At one point, yes, I was overweight. I would feed off of Mom's Italian dishes. Anything and everything from sausage bread on Christmas Eve, to never ending bowls of Pasta Fagioli. Mom's chicken cutlets would be considered a snack before dinner, and dessert was anything from cookies, to parfaits, to the occasional cannolis. I could never stop eating. I was always hungry and never satisfied. I was always tired. I even started experiencing severe allergy attacks at night due to my body's reaction to the different doses of medication. I was not in control.

One of the most annoying things about becoming a teenager is being surrounded by other teenagers. At this point in my life, it was the first time I began to get questioned about certain things. I dreaded wearing a bikini or showing my stomach in any shape or form. My friends or classmates would always ask, "Why do you have a second belly button?" Well, this "second belly button" is actually the scar from my Hydrocephalus. Then I would get questions like, "Did you have stomach surgery? If you have something wrong with your brain, why is your scar on your stomach?" These are the questions I never had to deal with before, and honestly, I didn't ever want to deal with them. But I would swallow the tears that I could feel coming and say, "I have some water on my brain, and in order for it to flush out, it goes through a tube down my stomach."

I would get stupid remarks from people—which I still get to this day—asking, "Why does your eye shift so much? Are you even looking at me?" All I would say in response was, "Yes. I am. But when I get overtired or stressed out, my eye shifts." One day, someone mistakenly touched the back of my head, felt the bump from my VP shunt, and screamed in shock because they thought something was seriously wrong. As annoyed as I felt, I would calmly say, "Don't worry, I've had it since I was born." I dreaded the days that I would have to leave early for my NYU doctor appointments because all the nosy classmates would ask why I leave school so often. I always hated having to explain myself.

I remember being about 13 years old. Having Italian genes while being on seizure medication meant having to deal with excessive body hair. Saying I was covered from head to toe in hair is an understatement. It was bad, and it was embarrassing. I was totally vulnerable to anything and everything anyone had to say at this point. After everything I had been through, I just wanted to be normal. I can clearly picture coming home one day and asking my mom who Chewbacca was. I told her that one of the boys at school told me I looked exactly like Chewbacca. My mom's face had this outraged look that I had never seen from her before. All she said was, "It's just a stupid movie character. Don't listen to those boys." But being the curious teenager that I was, I went straight to Google to look up what exactly this Chewbacca was. I was hurt, embarrassed, and even more internally angry than I had already been. Even when I was no longer having seizures, they were still controlling my life. (A year later, I would become one of the youngest teenagers to start painful laser hair removal treatments because the excessive arm, stomach, and back hair were uncontrollable.)

Little things started to bother me that never did before. I would get so anxious on gym days at school because I know I was the worst teammate. Gym class was the time when my limitations really shined through. I would always be picked last for a team, and when I was picked, I would hide in the back until class was over. I hated softball because when it was time to hit the ball, my skewed vision disabled me. I dreaded running around the bases and getting yelled at by classmates if I was going too slow. I was a fool. At one point, I was even on the cross country track team because I thought I would enjoy a sport where I was only competing against myself. To my surprise, I actually won the track award—but only for good team spirit.

The doctors would always tell my parents and me things that I should be aware of. Contact sports were out of the question because we never wanted to risk me getting hit in the head. For 22 years, I have never once been ice skating because I am too ashamed of having to wear a big clunky helmet on my head. Any fun school trips were always ruined for me because I would get too tired too fast, or I would always just have to be extra cautious with things. The kids at school thought my parents chaperoned the trips because they enjoyed it. However, truth be told, they had to be there to watch out for me.

I didn't want to explain why I am the way I am anymore. I was so young, yet so anxious, afraid, and unhappy. I know this probably sounds terrible, but I used to say to myself, "Why couldn't I be born with an obvious medical condition? Something that people would just understand? Something I didn't always have to explain." Being a teenager made me cringe at anything to do with Hydrocephalus or seizures. It was a thorn in my side that I was sick and tired of dealing with, and with high school around the corner, the last thing I wanted was to have to worry about my health.

Strength, Resilience, Growth

5 HIGH SCHOOL

Choosing the Right School

Being a Catholic School student means that you have probably been with the same classmates, took the same route, and wore the same clothes for 10+ years. With all the changes and bumps in the road in my childhood, the one thing that always stayed the same was the school I was in and the people I was surrounded by. However, as 8th grade rolled around, the next step was to look at high schools. It is kind of inevitable in Westchester County that if you go to Catholic grammar school, you end up in Catholic High school—most of which are either all-girls or all-boys schools.

There were always a handful of schools to choose from. However, first you had to do well enough on the TACHS exam--the Catholic high school entry exam--to be considered for any of them . Luckily, the girl who "might have severe learning disabilities" got accepted into every school she applied to. I will never forget opening my acceptance letter to Maria Regina High School. After visiting all the schools, none of them blew me away as much as Maria Regina, which is why I was beyond thrilled reading the words, "Congratulations and welcome to the class of 2016!"

Maria Regina is one of the many all-girl Catholic high schools in Westchester County. I remember walking into the open house and experiencing a sense of comfort, excitement, and maturity. For the most part, all of the high school open houses were the same. The cheerleaders would do their routines and get everyone excited with school spirit. The school principal would explain all of the academic opportunities and after-school programs the school had to offer. But there was one thing about Maria Regina that really stuck out to me—the award-winning choral ensemble. The first time I ever heard the glorious harmonies of this chorus, my eyes lit up, my heart beat fast, and I knew this was the place for me. From that moment on, no other school mattered. I was going to Maria Regina, and I was going to be in chorus.

Entering into high school was kind of a terrifying thought. Although I was excited for the change, I was also nervous. These nerves weren't your typical young teenager nerves. I was anxious about starting all over and having to constantly explain my disorders. And I was anxious about having to figure out new ways to hide my challenges when faced with new situations.

Despite my fears, my heart was still set on chorus. Even before my 8th-grade graduation, I had to audition for the choral ensemble if I wanted to be in it as a freshman. I remember leaving school early that day to get to Maria Regina in time for the audition. I had big, frizzy, curly hair due to the seizure medication and a really ugly unibrow. I was wearing baggy clothes because I didn't really own anything else besides a uniform. I was extremely worried because I had heard that, although very nice, the chorus teacher was tough and only chose the best of the best. I had practiced two audition pieces for months with my singing coach. She told me the best audition always includes a ballad and a song to show who you really are.

I can clearly picture waiting outside to be called into the audition. My heart was beating fast, and my anxiety was just as uncontrollable. I had to fill out a yellow sheet asking what two songs I'd be singing and whether I think I am an alto or a soprano. When the chorus teacher opened the door, I handed her the sheet and swallowed all of my nerves. She glanced at the paper, then up at me, in shock to learn that one of the pieces I would be performing was "Boogie Woogie Bugle Boy," a 1940s classic that no other 14-year-old girl would know.

I walked inside, stood behind the piano, and began to sing my choice for a ballad, "Somewhere Over the Rainbow." After about two verses, I was mortified when the teacher stopped the piano. I thought to myself, "Oh no, did I hit the wrong note? Did I say the wrong lyrics?" But to my surprise, all she said was, "Yeah, yeah, yeah, this song is a standard, but what I really want to hear is 'Boogie Woogie.' Now that's something different!"

I gave her a timid smile, barely said a word, and let my inner jazzy old soul get to work. My fingers started snapping while my feet were tapping. I kept my eyes closed as I always did when I would get into the song I was singing. I pictured myself as one of the Andrew Sisters standing in front of a big audience. When I finished the song and opened my eyes, reality struck, and it was just the chorus teacher and me. She gave me a little smile and politely told me that I will be hearing back early summer if I had made it in or not. She shook my hand, and that was it. Little did I know how she really felt about that audition, and that handshake was the start of a lifelong mentorship and friendship.

I went home kind of discouraged because I couldn't tell whether the teacher was pleased or not. At this time, 8th-grade graduation came and went, and summer rolled around. By mid-July, I was so excited to open my email, "rockgirl498" at the time, and see an email from Ms. Carozza. I was officially accepted into chorus. High school was going to be great.

The summer going into high school consisted of school supply shopping, new uniform fittings, and figuring out the best way to get to and from school each day. I remember going to pick up the train pass that I would use from now on instead of being driven to school. It was such a breath of fresh air knowing that I would be going to school every day with my best friends from elementary school instead of with my mom and dad.

I can clearly picture the first day of Maria Regina. So many thoughts ran through my head as I hopped on the train at the Fleetwood train station with many of my friends from childhood. This was so new to me. I wasn't sitting in the back seat of Mom's car anymore. I wasn't being watched every second of the day. I was officially a high school student.

Walking into Maria Regina for the first time was like walking into a whole new universe. There were faces of people I had never seen before. There were staircases, hallways, and classrooms that were not familiar. There was even a school gym, something my elementary school never had. I loved the way the school portrayed the Catholic faith. I enjoyed walking into the library and being able to actually use a computer in school. But what I enjoyed most was my first choral ensemble rehearsal. After waiting all summer to receive the acceptance email and then starting rehearsing, it felt so great sitting at the soprano end of the room, ready to prepare for my first concert. The first song I ever had to learn for chorus was, "He Aint Heavy, He's My Brother." I could already tell how much I was going to enjoy my time here because Ms. Carozza seemed just as much of an old soul as I was.

From the adventures on the train to the new classmates to the never-ending chorus harmonies, my first few weeks of high school were pretty great. My timid personality was able to flourish in chorus. However, as time went on, the rest of these four years were not as memorable.

Never Fully Fitting Into High School

I think the worst thing you could ever say to someone is, "High school is the best four years of your life, so you better make the most of it." It's hard having big expectations for something you really can't control. Even if you have a clear picture of how you expect your high school experience to go, it probably will take twists and turns and surprise you.

As high school started becoming more of a reality in my life, it also became something I was not physically, mentally, and emotionally able to handle. I didn't know how to respond to the idea of my old friends making new friends. I didn't know how to act at house parties or sporting events. I never knew the proper clothes to wear for school dances. And most importantly, I never knew how to explain myself when I couldn't take a sip of a beer because of my Hydrocephalus. I found myself choosing to stay home instead of going to any social events because deep down inside, I just wasn't comfortable. Sometimes I wouldn't even be able to explain why. Sometimes no one would even say anything to me to make me feel that way. However, sometimes I felt invisible because no one would say anything to me at all.

The exhilarating train ride was now dreadful. I went from sitting with all different people from local Catholic schools to standing in the corner because I just didn't fit in, and no one bothered to include me. I couldn't wrap my head around the "Friday night at the bar" conversations, or the never-ending gossip about whose Instagram picture was better. I didn't find things funny that other people did. I wasn't one to put loads of makeup on for all the Catholic school boys to see before the train ride home from school. I was an outcast.

Besides Ms. Carozza, there was one person who really helped me get through these four years. My best friend, Rosie. If you put Rosie and me in a room together and watched our personalities at best, you would probably wonder how the hell we became friends. Rosie was loud, funny, and confident, with a total "Don't fuck with me" attitude. I, on the other hand, was shy, quiet, and easily victimized. But here's the thing about Rosie and I. Despite our many differences, we have one thing in common that has bound us together for life. We both grew up with medical challenges and lived with fears, doctor's appointments, and undeserving teenage stressors. We had overprotective parents who had to know our every move, unlike the other girls who were able to do whatever they wanted. We also had kickass voices that made beautiful harmonies when we sang together.

I remember hoping at the start of each new school year that Rosie and I would have a class together besides chorus. I always felt a sense of comfort, knowing my best friend was by my side. She would help me make jokes about situations that would bring me down. Whenever I felt like I didn't fit in, she would give me a reason as to why I am so damn awesome.

***

Although she was my chorus teacher, I looked up to Ms. Carozza as more of a mentor. There was always this comfort and a sense of safety being around her. Each day before the bell rang for homeroom, while everyone else was gossiping in the cafeteria, I would walk in circles around the school because it was my only way of hiding. If I were lucky when I would walk by the chorus room, Ms. Carozza would be in there. We would talk about chorus, and she would ask me how I was doing. I would always be honest with her and say how I felt about being a shy high school student, but I still never really knew how to express myself. Ms. Carozza would always give me the best advice without overstepping any boundaries or hurting anyone's feelings.

Ms. Carozza had a lot of faith in me and my voice. She knew my voice had both a lot to sing and say, and she encouraged me to do so at every opportunity. She granted me some amazing solo pieces during chorus concerts such as, "An English Teacher," "Baby Please Come Home," and many show tunes. Each time I would either rehearse or perform a solo, my nerves would kick in full force. Instead of having shaky legs or butterflies in my stomach, my lips would always quiver uncontrollably, causing me to sing off-key. Although I loved to sing, I slowly but surely started to dread these performances. What I once thought was passion now only seemed like a hobby. I loved harmonizing with Rosie, but I wasn't getting the same amount of joy from it that I once was. I even started skipping out on some of my voice lessons because I just wasn't into it. But at this time, singing was still all I knew, so it was what I was going to do.

Despite my social challenges at this point in my life, I was flourishing in academics. Even with my Hydrocephalus, I was in AP classes, on the Dean's List, and becoming slightly obsessed with having perfect grades. This was definitely not what my parents expected, considering my condition and my dislike for studying and school work during elementary school. However, since I always felt so out of place, I found joy in studying hard and maintaining good grades.

Getting a Slight Introduction to Health

One year during high school, I was thrilled to find out that Ms. Carozza was going to be my health teacher. The girl who brought ham and cheese sandwiches on Italian bread with a side of Doritos to school definitely knew nothing about health. I was just happy to be around my favorite teacher more than once in the day. I don't remember much from health class because, quite frankly, I didn't really care. However, one day, the class had to watch a video about the meat products sold in America. I learned about how cows, chickens, and other animals are fed such terrible things, then slaughtered for us to eat. "So basically," I said disgustedly, "We are ingesting all of the bad stuff that these animals are eating?" I was mortified. I also learned the truth about how fast food places like McDonald's and Burger King process their meats. I came home that day and told my parents that we have to buy animals on a farm that are raised organically. Then we can store the meat in our freezer (which is too small and already stuffed with everything and anything). They looked at me like I had 10 heads and were completely confused about where this new interest of mine was coming from.

Sitting down for dinner during high school was probably my favorite part of the day. I would patiently wait in the kitchen as my mom prepared the meal for the night. I remember always tasting the food to "make sure it was ok." Meals usually consisted of chicken cutlets, pasta, mashed potatoes, meatballs, or zucchini pie, just to name a few. On Fridays, we would order from Joe's Pizzeria down the block, and I would easily devour at least three slices. However, these meals started changing as Mom decided to go on Weight Watchers. She began grilling chicken, baking potatoes, and slowly deviating from our usual dinner options. She even started weighing her portions, which I thought was so weird. My mom would sit at the dinner table and count how many "points" the meal was. To lose the weight she wanted, she needed to stick to a certain number of points.

As ridiculous as I thought this was, I started to see all the positive results my mom was getting from this plan. I had never really had a self-image problem. Still, I knew now that my seizure medication was over and I was getting older, it was important to start getting healthy. I was still slightly overweight due to years of uncontrollable eating, so I told my mom I wanted to follow her on this plan. She was supportive and excited that this could be something we could do together.

I would always ask my mom to cook spaghetti instead of ziti. This was because a cup of spaghetti was a bigger portion and way more filling than the ziti. I even started counting how many points chocolate bars and peanut butter and jelly sandwiches would be. Although I didn't quite grasp the point of the diet yet, I started to become mindful of portion control. So what if I was still eating Reese's peanut butter cheesecake? At least I only had seven points worth! I even started having cinnamon and brown sugar oatmeal every morning instead of my daily Eggo waffles.

In addition to introducing healthier foods into my diet, my mom took this opportunity to encourage more physical activity. I was 16 years old when she brought me to the gym for the first time. I remember always pulling up after school, thinking, "Why am I here?" My mom would make me go on the treadmill with her, and all I would think about was what was for dinner. But despite my hesitation with the gym, I actually started to enjoy it. I liked seeing some results on my body, and I loved having something physical I could do. But at this point, fitness was just a thing to do and not a further thought in my mind. I still would jump for joy when I had chorus practice and wouldn't be able to make it to the gym.

Being an "Upperclassman"

When you are a freshman in high school, all you look forward to is climbing up the ladder to becoming an upperclassman. In my last two years of high school, I felt as though I wasn't really a victim anymore, however, I wasn't anywhere near confident. I spent my days studying, singing, and going to the gym with my mom after school. I wasn't as bothered by my early high school experience as I used to be, but I was still antisocial, shy, and ready to graduate.

In my junior year, I was introduced to a new club the school offered, gospel choir. I was thrilled because now, in addition to chorus, I had another singing group to get me through the days. In gospel choir, the instructor taught us many songs that were sung at school masses to portray the Catholic faith. I enjoyed how these songs made me feel more and more connected to my spirituality. Rosie and I would come up with all different harmonies, and we would look forward to singing at every first Friday Mass at school. Although I always had chorus to help me feel a sense of community, gospel choir also gave me a purpose.

I remember one day getting up to leave after gospel choir rehearsal was over. I was a senior at this point. I can still hear my instructor say to me, "Sophia, wait a minute. You didn't seem like yourself today. Is everything OK?" I was comfortable enough to talk to him about what I was feeling. All I said was, "As my last few months of high school are approaching, I still don't understand why I feel so lost. Aren't you supposed to find yourself in high school? Why do I feel like I don't fit in anywhere I turn?" My instructor looked at me and said, "Sophia, you don't fit in. I bet you feel like you should have been born in a different time. I can see how you are different from others. But you DO have a purpose. I know for a fact that you were put here, at this time, to change the world. Even if you feel out of place, you will find your place, and you will make the world a better place. You have not found your calling yet. I bet you music isn't even it. But I am certain you are going to do something amazing, I can see the light of God in you." I was so taken aback.

I didn't know how to respond. But those words have stuck with me ever since.

My last few months of high school were filled with college prep meetings, SAT testing, college visits, and a ton of stress. In an ideal world, I would go to school to be a singer and come out to be the next star on Broadway. However, this was not realistic, and my over-achieving academic success would not be going to waste. I decided I wanted to go to college to be an engineer. Not because I truly wanted to build stuff, but because I thought that maybe there was a way to integrate math and science with music. So I decided to go to Manhattan College to become a mechanical engineer in hopes of creating music equipment in the future. This all sounded great and extremely attainable. However, was it what I truly wanted? If you had asked me back then, I would have said that this path was my dream. But I wouldn't have been able to explain why or how.

As prom and graduation rolled around and all the other girls were excited for their big trips to the Bahamas or the Jersey shore, Rosie and I had other plans. Sure, it was fun to get dressed up and go to prom. It was even pretty awesome at graduation when I won the music award. However, nothing was more important than what Rosie and I had in mind. We were going to do whatever it took for our parents to let us spend a week alone in California—and boy, did it take a lot.

6 CALIFORNIA

At 18 years old, I never had a sleepover. I never spent a night anywhere without my mom and dad. I never stayed up past midnight because, due to my Hydrocephalus and seizure disorder, I always needed my rest. And I never had a desire to spend a week away at the beach like all the other girls I graduated with. What can I say? I am different. I've always wanted different experiences, but by no means was I ever comfortable enough to go for them. I wouldn't even dare entertain the thought of going away to college.

I look back at high school and appreciate the adventurous moments that I allowed myself to have, most of which Rosie talked me into. I remember those last few months at Maria Regina when Rosie and I sat at the lunch table discussing how we weren't allowed to have a big after-prom trip like the other girls. We weren't upset about it because we didn't really want one anyway. Rosie and I weren't friends with the whole school, we did our own thing. So why would we want to spend an uncomfortable week away with all our classmates? However, we wanted to take the first steps into the music business before college started. Luckily, I have an uncle who lives in the heart of the music world, and once Rosie got wind of this, there was no turning back. Sophia and Rosie were going to take on California.

We would sit in the cafeteria looking up hotel locations and flight prices as if we got approval from our parents. We decided one day that it was time to have "the talk." I could feel my stomach turning as I was getting ready to have this conversation with my parents. This was the first time I ever asked anything this big from them—and I knew they would probably say no.

After many family sit-downs, long hours of research on safe locations, and many phone calls with my uncle, our parents finally agreed to let me and Rosie take a once-in-a-lifetime trip to California. If Rosie or I were any other kid, our parents probably wouldn't even think twice about the trip. But due to our histories, the day we hopped on that plane was the most emotional moment for our parents. We probably gave each of them about 10 hugs, and reassured them that we would call them every day before we got to leave the state.

When we finally got to California, the first thing Rosie and I wanted to do was see the Hollywood sign, because we were definitely going to be Hollywood stars. We got to see numerous landmarks around Los Angeles, such as the Hollywood walk of fame, Rodeo Drive, and the Santa Monica Pier, thanks to my uncle. We stayed in the most beautiful, 5-star hotel, and definitely took advantage of room service.

At this point in my life, I really started to follow certain habits and rituals, even being away on vacation. It was the first time ever that I started having my own routine. One that I was in control of. I felt that California was the perfect time for me to start dictating how I wanted to live my life. Interestingly enough, this routine included eating a healthy breakfast and exercising. Two things that had nothing to do with why I was in California to begin with. Every morning on the trip, I would wake up super early before the sun rose, get dressed, make a bowl of oatmeal in the hotel room, and make my way down to the hotel gym (which, by the way, is my morning routine to this day). I would do beginner weight training exercises I learned from being around people at the gym, then I would hop on the treadmill. I really enjoyed this part of the day because, as an only child, although I loved spending time with Rosie, I was not used to sharing my personal space.

After we would get ready for the day, my uncle would pick us up, take us around town, then bring us to his house to record music all day. My memories of professionally recording will always bring me joy. Listening back to my own original song, "Got These Feels," and the many covers that Rosie and I recorded, makes me think about how this trip was really one of a lifetime. Spending hours in a recording studio, eating Chipotle for dinner, and losing all track of time seemed entertaining. Still, I started to get this uneasy feeling about all of these experiences. At the time, I didn't realize why this was happening, or even that it was happening at all. I was almost let down by this lifestyle. It was discouraging to meet so many people "trying to make it." I really didn't enjoy this culture. Did I really picture myself doing this for the rest of my life? What if I don't make it as a singer? Do I see myself working long hours every night just to make some extra cash? What if engineering musical equipment isn't actually a real thing? But in pure SRG fashion, I pushed these thoughts back into my head and tried my hardest not to address them.

Once the trip was over and it was time to go home, I was sad but ready to move on. I remember being so excited to get back in the gym. To meet up with some of the local gym rats I had become friendly with so that I could learn more about weightlifting. For the first time ever, this was all I could think about. The gym.

***

When I got home, it was still only the beginning of July. I had the whole summer ahead of me before college. I started it out on such a positive note and was determined to end it even better. I was still spending my summer days at Beckwith Pointe, just not as a little girl anymore. The never ending games of manhunt, the night swimming, and the Friday night DJ were the same as they had always been.

But something was happening. These things didn't seem to excite me the way they used to anymore. Instead of hanging around friends at the beach club, I found myself always huddled in a corner alone. For some reason, I was miserable. Everyone around me probably had their own opinions as to why I was like this. Did something happen in California? Is Sophia scared to go to college? Is there something medically wrong with her? On top of the depressing state I was in and the numerous concerns of others, I started getting sick from certain foods. I remember everyone thinking I was crazy and probably just overreacting. But the stomach pains and digestive problems I would have after eating any type of bread or pasta was definitely not me overreacting. My newfound gluten allergy did not pair well with my unexplainable emotional state. I was fed up with everything and everyone.

I didn't know it back then, but California was both the best and worst experience of my life. It was amazing for a number of reasons, including my memories with Rosie and newfound independence. I was finally on my own. But it also felt like the worst because it showed me that what I thought I wanted my whole life was actually not something I desired at all. And I was not about to settle. Although the freedom I got to experience seemed bittersweet, it was also something I didn't know how to handle. Was I really ready to let go of the boundaries of my childhood?

The only thing at this point that brought me joy and took me away from my feelings was the gym. I began to learn how to properly structure an exercise program. The never ending minutes on the treadmill started to get cut down as I learned other effective ways to workout. I wasn't just in the gym because my mom forced me anymore. I was there because I was hooked. The girl who couldn't walk or run was now learning how to squat, deadlift, and sprint. My imbalances were still a challenge as I learned new things (and still are), but I loved it. I loved seeing what my body could do after years of doing nothing. I enjoyed the sense of community I felt at the gym, like I finally fit in somewhere.

My desire to spend hours at the beach club subsided. Now, I was occupied by working out and educating myself on the human body. I completely changed that summer, but as college was right around the corner and I found a new hobby, it was time to focus on a new chapter.

Strength, Resilience, Growth

7 COLLEGE

Starting College at Manhattan

The idea of college for any young adult is exhilarating. You get to live away from home, finally study something of interest, and basically do whatever you want without anyone stopping you. College is the time for endless parties, late-night outings, binge drinking, microwavable dinners, and complete independence. All of which sounds great for the average 18-year-old.

Maybe that's why I never got any of these feelings towards college. Was I average? At 18, I was completely disgusted, ashamed, and mad about everything I ever had to go through up until this point. In my head, I totally wanted to be average, even though I knew I wasn't. So, I constantly convinced myself that I was. That none of those horrible experiences ever happened to me. That no one would ever have to know how I felt during that first seizure, or the EEG tests, or the dreadful physical therapy appointments. If I had managed to hide all of this throughout my years at Maria Regina, there was no reason I couldn't do it again in college.

My first day of college was quite untraditional. I didn't get there hours or days before to decorate my dorm room, nor was I hanging out with any sororities. Instead, I woke up at 5:50am, got dressed, brushed my teeth, ate my big bowl of oatmeal with a special spoon I had once gotten from my grandma, and headed to the same local gym I had been going to since high school for my morning workout. As a commuter, I only had to be on campus when I had class. And that's really the only time I ever wanted to be there. I remember the first day of college seeming like any other day for me. It was a Tuesday, which meant "back day," according to my workout schedule. I wasn't concerned about my new class schedule or any possible extra-curricular activities I could get involved with. I wasn't excited about going to college the way Rosie or any of my other friends were. I was more concerned with hitting a new personal record with deadlifts and making sure my morning workout was completed.

I never really wanted to go to Manhattan in the first place, but it was the only local college with a kickass engineering program. I remember driving into school, parking my car in the overcrowded parking lot, and trying to navigate where my first class of the day was. I would walk past girls and guys I was acquainted with during high school, but of course, felt like the invisible outcast as I barely got a wave hello. The first day, I sat down in my calculus class surrounded by other girls from my old high school. These girls were never particularly mean to me, which is why I felt let down as they would turn their heads away and pretend as if they had not known me for the past four years. Unfortunately, I was used to this treatment at this point, so much so that I didn't really care. I was excited to make new friends and hopefully, new exciting memories.

My first year of college consisted of classes like calculus, chemistry, physics, engineering 101, and many science-based lab classes. Unfortunately, the engineering students really only had classes together, so it was hard to make a diverse group of friends. I thought it would be a good idea to audition for the acapella group at school. Compared to my high school chorus audition, I wasn't nervous nor enthusiastic about this one. However, as I almost expected, my kickass pipes granted me a soprano spot in acapella. At first, acapella was pretty fun. I've always loved the harmonic sounds of different voices coming together to make beautiful music. But after only a few weeks of practice and participating in just one acapella concert, I started really dreading rehearsals. I didn't feel that sense of community the way I did with Maria Regina's chorus. I wasn't fitting in with the rest of the acapella group. The students were all very competitive, and I didn't feel the joy of the music. Maybe it was me, though. My desire to sing wasn't as strong as it used to be. I began skipping practice because it interfered with my gym time. I wasn't choosing one thing over the other. But I was finally choosing to put myself into situations that made me feel comfortable. With acapella not doing that for me, I decided to quit and just focus on my engineering degree.

Calculus and physics weren't the same as they were in high school. I was always good at math, so I was still maintaining good grades. I understood the basics of physics, but all the extra engineering crap made no sense to me. I remember one of the professors asked us to use our new knowledge to build a bridge using engineering software. When calculus and physics were put in real-life situations, I was totally lost. I was also bored out of my mind. I remember sitting in class with all the other engineering students feeling dumbfounded. They would get together and come up with all these ideas to create new and effective technology. The only thing I was really interested in creating was my workout for the following day.

I Got the Best Christmas Gift During College

I always say that as an only child, my parents didn't raise me to be a spoiled person. However, they did raise me as a spoiled child. I wasn't given any gas money when it was time to fill up my car. I had to get my first job at 15 years old to learn the value of saving and spending money. And when it was time to go out shopping with friends, I never even dared to ask my parents for money. They raised me to learn how to work for what I wanted. However, when it came time for Christmas, my birthday, or any other big holiday or event, I was definitely the spoiled child. My parents always make Christmas such a joyous time for my family and me. On Christmas Eve, we celebrate with the Italian tradition of the feast of the seven fishes. Our tiny little apartment becomes the center for endless food, laughs, and unforgettable memories. We enjoy everything from my mom's sausage bread and spaghetti with clam sauce, to Italian Christmas cookies. On Christmas Day, the apartment is quiet and reminiscent of the night before, and my mom puts together a beautiful display of presents under the tree signed, "Love, Santa."

Every year, I always have one "big finale" gift. It is usually in a big box or hidden somewhere in the back of the tree. But one year during college, my parents' "big finale" gift was small and wrapped in a little bit of tissue paper. I remember thinking to myself, "THIS? THIS IS THE BIG FINALE??" My mom could see how upset I was, but didn't say anything. She knew that just like every other year, I would not be disappointed. I ripped open the tissue paper to find a piece of paper. I turned it around and read, "'Merry Christmas! This grants you six personal training sessions!'"I was shocked, thrilled, and extremely grateful for this gift. I couldn't believe my parents thought to do this. I loved it so much that I couldn't put any words together to express my exhilaration. I closed my eyes and said to myself, "Wow this new hobby of mine is finally becoming more of a reality. If mom and dad notice how important it is to me then it must be special!" I was finally going to learn proper exercise technique, and really challenge my body on what it could do after all these years of feeling limited. Even though I had already started formulating a workout plan for myself, it was going to be cool to have proper guidance. I remember thinking how funny it was that I was excited to be getting a personal trainer to boss me around with physical fitness, when I hated every minute of physical therapy!

My first personal training appointment was one that I will never forget. The trainer first assessed me to check my form, abilities, and the things I needed to work on. Even though I had been exercising for some time now, my nerves were really kicking in. This was the first time since physical therapy that someone else was manipulating my body to do what it was supposed to do. Although the lump in my throat and the butterflies in my stomach were unsettling, I didn't hate this guidance as much as physical therapy. Instead, I was ready to see what I needed to do to improve my performance in what I like to consider my sport.

The first thing we worked on and continued to work on during each session was squats. I like to consider squats my enemy. A constant reminder of my imbalances. I got so frustrated when learning how to properly squat because it took me forever to keep my heels on the ground. I was incapable of evenly distributing my weight to get the most benefits out of the exercise. The trainer would always say, "Don't put pressure on your tippy-toes. It's all in your heels." This infuriated me as it reminded me of all those times Myrielle worked on getting me to walk on my heels. Despite my chosen career path and my growing knowledge and technique with exercise, I can honestly say that squats are still my biggest challenge. But I wasn't going to let that stop me then or now.

Besides squats, my trainer taught me many valuable things. I was excited to learn about different set and rep combinations and how to work out each muscle group effectively. I felt most powerful during any upper body workout days because that's where my strength flourished. And anything that made me feel strong made me happy.

Feeling Confused Halfway Through Freshman Year

All my friends thought it was so ambitious to choose such a hard major. And everyone in my family would always brag about my career choice and how smart I was. But there I was, a second semester engineering student, an acapella group dropout, the only college freshman who brought lunch to school because I wanted to make my own healthy options, and bored out of my mind. I dreaded the three-hour lab classes and the long lectures about how to effectively change the world with modern-day engineering techniques. It wasn't until the end of January 2017 that I made one of the biggest decisions of my academic career.

It was a cold, dreary night, and I had just gotten home from an endless physics lab. I wasn't excited about being home because it meant I had to study for my physics test, which was the next day. I could tell I was losing all motivation for engineering because as hard as physics was, I had left it until the last minute. And anyone who knows SRG knows that procrastination is not in her vocabulary.

I only had a few hours to study because I wanted to get up at my normal time to do my workout, despite the importance of this test. I sat down with a pit in my stomach, opened the book, and started seeing what seemed like another language on the paper. I was completely lost. So lost that I didn't even have the motivation to figure out what I wasn't understanding. Instead, my heart started beating fast, tears welled up in my eyes, and I screamed out, "I can't do this anymore!!!!!" My parents rushed into my room to see what was wrong, and I finally broke down about how I was feeling. Any other parent would tell me to stop putting it off and study hard. But from the start, my parents knew engineering wasn't where my heart was. At the time, none of us really knew what I was supposed to do, but engineering wasn't it.

But even though I felt so lost with engineering, I knew what I wanted. I wanted to do something in the health field. I wasn't quite sure what, but I was ready to switch my major into health sciences. I spent that whole night researching on Manhattan College's website the different health degrees they offer. I totally dismissed that physics test and proudly received my first ever big fat "F"! I scrolled across the school's "Allied Health Sciences" degree, and right off the bat, I was interested. Within just 24 hours, I went into the department dean's office, gained all the information about the program, and learned that these credits could lead me to become a nutritionist. I never actually thought about myself as a nutritionist, but at that moment, I got this positive, invigorating, feeling as if I knew this was for me. All I had to do was finish out the year, maintaining solid grades in the most dreaded major. Then I could finally do something I was excited about

8 HOW PERSONAL TRAINING FOUND ME

February 9, 2017

In New York, February is one of the most dreaded months of the year. Although only a short month, the days give minimal hours of sunlight, and the temperature is usually cold enough to freeze your ass off. I've always hated February. I've always despised the winter. But I've always looked forward to snow days from school because it meant I got to stay home, watch movies, and drink hot chocolate all day.

February 9, 2017 is probably not a day most people remember. It was a random day in the middle of winter with cold winds, dark and lifeless skies, and snow-covered grounds. I remember this day clearly because it was the first time I ever hated a snow day. Sure, I was off from school and didn't have to get out of my pajamas all day, but my only concern at this point was if the gym were open or not. It was a Thursday, which meant that it was that time of the week to hit chest and shoulders. I was finally starting to use heavier weights, perform harder sets, and take shorter rest periods while working out, and I was not going to let a snow day hinder my progress. However, this wasn't just a normal snow day. It was a blizzard. A heavy-wind, low-visibility blizzard dropping so much snow that it was almost impossible to walk out the front door. But who cares? In my mind, I kept telling myself that the gym was only a few miles away, and if I got stuck on the car ride there, I could just walk the rest of the way. Even if it was snowing like crazy and below zero degrees. No big deal.

I made it a point to leave the house around 5am when my parents were still asleep and unable to stop me. My overly ambitious attitude took me right to my little bright red Volkswagen Jetta. The Jetta was the car I was driving at the time and could be picked out by anyone miles away. It took me on many adventures as a new driver and kept me safe. But this snowy drive to the gym was definitely going to be a challenge. As I was driving, I could barely see out the window. However, I wasn't scared. I was extremely calm and in my own thoughts. I kept my eyes on the road, two hands on my wheel, and my foot easily riding the break, just as my dad would have told me to do. I slid a few times here and there, but I would take a deep breath and say out loud, "God, if you get me here safely, I promise I will do something so great and so worthwhile." Little did I know what he really had in store for me.

I managed to get myself into the snow-covered gym parking lot. There was only one other car there, which belonged to the manager of the gym at the time. I got out of the car and lugged myself and my big clunky snow boots into the gym. The manager was the only one working the front desk and looked at me like I was nuts. Because let's face it, I was. As I took off all my snow gear and looked around at the empty gym, I was so excited to have every single piece of machinery all to myself. I didn't have to wait for anyone to finish or rush through my sets to let someone else have a turn. And if I got stuck there because of the snow, at least I had everything I needed for a workout. I ended up having one of the best workouts I had ever had. I was so focused on my chest presses, my shoulder raises, and every other exercise I performed that day. As I was finishing up, I can clearly picture the manager coming towards me. He was wearing a big, warm flannel shirt and khakis. He asked me if I would come into his office to speak with him. Due to my generalized anxiety, so many thoughts were going through my mind. As I followed him inside, I kept hearing voices in my head saying, "Oh no, did I break one of the machines? Is he going to tell me to leave? Did someone complain about me?"

I sat down, crossed my legs, and started tapping my foot uncontrollably. He looked at me with a smirk and said, "Sophia, relax." After I took a deep breath, he blurted out something I was not expecting whatsoever. "Sophia look—you work out here harder than anyone I have ever seen. I mean, look at you. You're here during a blizzard! And you're good. And people want to work out like you. They want to work out with you. They constantly ask me if the tiny girl with strong muscles and determination can train them. But I always say no because you are not a certified trainer." I looked at him in almost disbelief because I really had no idea where he was going with this. "My point is, whatever it is that you're doing with your life right now, are you happy? Because I think you would be an amazing personal trainer and I know it would make you happy. Which is why the gym will offer you the employee discount to get certified and then start working here as your first training experience. Is this something you would be interested in?" Without any hesitation, I jumped up out of the seat, looked him straight in the eye, and said, "How do I get this done, and when do I start?" I could feel my heart beating in a way it has never beat before. Like something amazing was about to happen. He handed me a bright piece of paper to be filled out. I looked at it with awe. Like I finally found my calling, my true love.

It was still snowing hard while driving home from the gym, but the trip seemed a lot less stressful. I was relaxed because I got my workout in, and I was beyond excited about how my future was about to unfold. I rushed upstairs into the apartment. Before I could even take my clunky snow boots and big heavy North Face coat off, I slammed the paper on the dining room table for my mom to see. "MOM! MOM!" I eagerly shouted. "THE MANAGER AT THE GYM WANTS ME TO BECOME A PERSONAL TRAINER AND WILL HIRE ME TO WORK THERE AS MY FIRST JOB! CAN I DO IT?" At this point, my mom knew how important fitness was becoming in my life, and with the decision to change majors, it only seemed fitting.

At that moment, nothing phased me. It didn't matter that the snow kept coming down, covering the streets of Gramatan Avenue, or that the heat was barely working in our apartment. What mattered was signing myself up for the online personal training course. I logged onto the website to get started in the process. As I read the words, "This certification will take about six months to complete," my inner ambition thought differently. There was no way this was going to take me six months. I felt determined enough to get this done much quicker, even if it was the only thing I did for the next few weeks or so.

From that point forward, my personal training studies were all that mattered. I would study before the gym at 5am, and I would study during my workout and test myself on which muscles I was using. I would take online quizzes and practice tests for my dream certification with any spare moment I had, even between my college classes.

Studying to Be a Trainer

During my studies, I met one of the trainers I had frequently seen but never talked to at the gym. I was always a bit intimidated by Kim. Her bubbly personality, over-the-top energy, and knowledge about exercise made me nervous to talk to her. She kind of reminded me of Rosie. Very outgoing and totally confident in what she knew and who she was. At this point in my life, although high school had long ended and I finally found something I was confident about, I was still shy and unable to express my thoughts and feelings. When Kim got word that I was becoming a personal trainer, she welcomed me with open arms. She was excited that the gym was going to have another girl on the team and that someone with my passion for exercise was going to be able to help others. Despite my uncertainty about Kim's personality at first, she and I hit it off instantly. I would ask her questions regarding my personal training studies. She would constantly check my form on exercises I was unsure about, and she always managed to build up my confidence whenever I was nervous about my test.

Throughout all of February and March, Kim helped me with proper training techniques. She even introduced me to clients she thought would be a perfect fit for me once I was certified. She really took me under her wing and made sure that I was going to be the best personal trainer I could be. Her constant support and motivation made me even more eager to complete my certification.

As my studies progressed and I started feeling more knowledgeable about the science behind exercise, I decided it was time to set a date for my certification test. I remember logging online to see two possible dates. One was very soon while the other was months away. I chose the closest date. Wednesday, April 5, 2017. What better way to spend my 19th birthday than to start the first steps of what could be a lifelong, life-changing career.

Even though I was thrilled about what I was doing, I really didn't tell many people. My dad always told me to "Go forth and tell no one." To focus on the task at hand before getting other people's opinions involved. I still follow this advice today. There was one person, however, that I did tell. For some reason, I couldn't wait to tell the owner of the spa I go to. Adriana has been waxing my eyebrows since I was about 13 years old with the big fat unibrow. She has made sure my eyebrows have been perfect for every big event or just my everyday life. Adriana has always been like family to me. She supports any decisions I make, she praises my excellent work ethic, and she always makes sure I look my best for whatever life throws my way. When I explained to Adriana that I was studying to be a personal trainer, she was just as thrilled as I was. She even suggested that I "practice" my training techniques using her as a client. So that's what I did. Twice a week at night, I went to the empty spa once it closed to train Adriana. We would squeeze ourselves into one of the massage rooms because, although small, it was conducive enough for what we needed to do. There was nothing like exercising with eucalyptus scents in the background! I would assess Adriana's physical fitness and help her with certain everyday movements she struggled with. I really made her fall in love with moving her body. My experience training Adriana gave me a sense of purpose. Like personal training and I were meant to be.

***

One of my biggest pet-peeves is having anyone talk to me during my workout. I am always so focused on what I have to do. I treat my time working out as my solitary time. It is when I get to strengthen not only my body but also my mind, soul, and spirit. However, as a future trainer, I needed to get used to having people talk to me during this time. My first experience dealing with someone who constantly loved interrupting my workout was with a man named Jimi. Jimi was one of Kim's clients at the time. He always took it upon himself to talk to me during my workout. When I first met Jimi, his overly-friendly self really annoyed me. I didn't want to be bothered. Jimi is extremely rough around the edges. He is the type of guy who will ride his motorcycle in shorts and a tank top in sub-zero temperatures. Jimi is covered in tattoos, extremely tall, has crazy curly hair, and lives without a filter. Whatever he thinks, he says. Even if it is when I am covered in sweat, out of breath, and unapproachable.

But if I was ever guilty of judging a book by its cover, it was when I first met Jimi. After just a few weeks of knowing me, Jimi would always take it upon himself to buy me tea if it was a cold morning, or make sure my car was running smoothly. He really looked out for me, especially when I would be one of the only young girls at the gym, surrounded by all the big muscle heads. Although annoying, Jimi's commentary was always quite funny. While it took some time to get used to his banter, I actually started growing fond of him. I got a kick out of when he would call me "Hercules" because of how heavy I lifted. It made me feel powerful, especially since it was coming from a man like him! He eventually got the hint that I hated talking during my workouts, so he would just wave to me and wait until I was done before asking me any questions.

Although we had not known each other very long, Jimi would always bust my chops just like he does to this day. He would constantly tell me I look like a man when I work out, or that I am too short. But his comments never bothered me. Instead, they helped build my confidence. They made me fight back. I found myself starting to throw really clever comebacks his way whenever he would say something about me. We would laugh, and he would say, "There ya go! You are finally growing a pair!"

Jimi had been working with Kim due to many of his past shoulder injuries. However, he would become one of my very first clients because Kim trusted me enough to help him with his limitations. At this point, Jimi couldn't wait for me to be his trainer. And honestly, neither could I.

April 5, 2017

I have always made it a point to make each birthday special since that ninth birthday at the American Girl Store. When I turned 16, I went to Hershey Park and spent the whole weekend making my own chocolate bars. (And yes, at that point, I made sure the chocolate bar fit within my Weight Watchers points allowance for the day.) At 17, I convinced myself it was a special birthday because of the numerous amount of songs written about 17-year-olds. By the time I turned 18, it was special because I was technically an "adult." And now, on April 5, 2017, my 19th birthday was going to be the day I became a trainer.

I normally wake up every day with some level of anxiety, but nothing could compare to the amount I had that morning. It was a Wednesday, which meant I didn't have to go to my college class until the late afternoon. My usual 5:50am alarm went off, and I did my daily morning routine before the gym. I made sure to get an amazing leg day in before taking my certification test. I remember exercising that morning and getting so frustrated with myself. I felt like my squats were terrible, my Romanian deadlifts weren't straight enough, and my rest periods were too long. But I was just overthinking and getting myself even more anxious for this test.

My mom drove me to the testing center in one of the local towns in Westchester. We walked inside, and my mom gave me a big hug saying, "Sophia, you got this. I love you." I signed into the testing site and was seated at one of the computers. I took a deep breath and thought about how this test could be the start of a new beginning. I pressed "start test" as my hand was uncontrollably shaking and got to work. Surprisingly, once I started the test, I was a lot more relaxed. I flew through most of the multiple-choice questions, only getting stumped on ones that I knew I was overthinking. It took me about an hour before I got to the final question. Once I clicked "finish test," my anxiety kicked back in. I watched the little circle load on the screen in front of me. The 30 seconds that it took to fully load my results felt like a lifetime. My heart was beating out of my chest, my palms were covered in sweat, and my head started pounding. Finally, the words I had been waiting to see popped up on the screen, "Congratulations, on April 5, 2017, you have passed with a grade of 97% and are now a certified personal trainer." It felt so surreal. I couldn't believe I passed the exam. On my first try. With a 97%. I ran out of the testing center with the printed certification in hand, found my mom in the waiting room, and screamed out, "THIS IS THE BEST BIRTHDAY EVER!"

The first thing I did before going to class that day was drive to the gym in the pouring rain to tell the manager I had passed. He was shocked that it had taken me less than two months but excited to get me on board. I called Jimi right away to tell him the news. His way of congratulating me was saying, "You are such an overachiever. Who gets a 97% on the first try?"

I felt like a total badass, as I was given my first trainer shirt. I put it on and was ready to conquer this new career. I was nervous about having others trust their bodies with me, but I knew I would not disappoint. At that moment, I had no idea that personal training would take me to where I am today.

9 MY CORE FOUR

The Early Lessons Learned

Ever since childhood, I've always had to experience things that others my age didn't. I've been told I am "wise beyond my years." I had to mentally grow up faster than most to deal with all the stress in my early life. During my first year as a trainer, my older mentality really shined through. I learned a lot of physical, mental, and emotional skills, most of which any other 19-year-old wouldn't be able to handle. My co-workers were all at least double my age. They had years of experience under their belt. I was the youngest trainer at the gym but was somehow always able to fit in and be treated as an equal. I was now given opportunities to train people of different ages, personalities, ethnicities, physical limitations, and disabilities. While others my age were going to bars on the weekends or staying up late to binge-watch Netflix, I was making phone calls to potential clients, setting up my weekly schedule, or coming up with new workout ideas for people. But I didn't mind. I absolutely loved it.

Although I started to develop a reputation as the fitness queen at the gym, at first, I found it difficult to sell myself as a trainer. I would do a few free assessment sessions for people and nail it, but then completely lose any train of thought when trying to sell them future sessions. I was talking with Kim one day, and the words that came out of her mouth have never left my mind since. "Sophia, I've never seen anyone with a passion for training like you. You are so young, yet I know you will go so far with this. But sweetie, high school is over, and this isn't college. You're not a kid anymore. Even though you are only 19, you are now working as an adult, and you need to show that confidence. You cannot be shy if you want to make it in this business. You have the passion, but now you need the assurance. Go out there, and get them!!" Her words resonated with me as I knew I needed to take her advice. It was time to shine and not let any of my past experiences cause me any uncertainty in my work.

The most exciting thing for a new personal trainer is finally gaining clients. If I told you that the second you become a trainer, you automatically have a ton of people who want to train with you, I would definitely be lying. But here's the cool thing about me. I believe that if you practice what you preach and walk your talk, you get results. And that's exactly what happened. Since I worked out at the gym, and people saw the hard work I put into keeping my own body strong and healthy, they instantly wanted to train with me. They knew I was serious and would provide them with amazing results.

DANIELLE

My first official client, besides Jimi, of course, was Danielle, a school psychologist in her mid-thirties. Naturally, as a trainer, you want to help clients get on a sustainable, healthy lifestyle. You hope that they will want to incorporate fitness into their daily routine. However, Danielle was adamant that she was only going to train for a few months to look her best for her friend's wedding. Although Danielle dreaded our nightly sessions and occasionally complained about the exercises I would give her, the determination she showed was unimaginable. She never missed a session. She did every exercise, no matter how hard it was. And most importantly, she trusted me. I like to believe that although I was the one with the credentials, Danielle trained me to be a better coach. She was the first client to ever do full hour sessions with me. Sometimes, as I would run out of ideas during the last few minutes of each workout, Danielle would say something like, "C'mon Sophia, we have two more minutes. Let me just do sit-ups!" We created a bond almost instantly. She helped me bring the fun into fitness. To not treat every workout so seriously. She treated me as if I was her age. As a matter of fact, she was completely blown away when she found out I was only 19. "You're only 19! How can that be? I thought you were in your mid to late 20s! You are so mature and have such a solid head on your shoulders," she would say. From planks to push-ups to never ending squats, Danielle was the best first client anyone could ask for. She was also the first woman besides Rosie, that I felt like I could be myself around. And, little did I know at the time, she would become one of the greatest friends.

By mid-April of 2017, I had now been doing multiple sessions. Some free assessment sessions never turned into any sales. Still I was too occupied with Jimi and Danielle to get upset about it. Jimi and I worked on his shoulder mobility, his strength gains, and his posture. I found myself always yelling at him to keep his back straight, to squat down on his heels, and to keep his knees aligned. Danielle and I were determined to get her in shape for her friend's wedding. I also worked hard to strengthen her back muscles because, as it turns out, she had a very bad case of scoliosis.

JENELLE

I've always loved Saturdays at the gym because I feel less rushed and more relaxed, and everyone else seems to have the same mindset. Everyone's workouts are better because they aren't squeezing in their last rep before work, or trying to share a bunch of machines during the 5pm rush-hour crowd. I'll never forget one beautiful Saturday morning that April. I had just finished my workout and was ready to train a new client who had booked an assessment with me. I was standing at the front of the gym when this tall girl, about 5'7", with big brown hair, designer sunglasses, and a slick leather jacket walked in. As she went to check in with the front desk, all I heard her say was, "Hi, I'm Jenelle, and I am here for my session with Sophia." I could feel my stomach start to turn and my face getting red. I wasn't normally nervous for a new client, but there was something about Jenelle that caught me off guard. Deep down, I knew this was not going to be just another one-time client. I knew I had to give Jenelle the most amazing workout because I felt like at that moment, she was given to me as a client for a reason.

My first session with Jenelle is one I will never forget. She was wearing new bright white Adidas sneakers that she bought for her new fitness journey. When I asked her what her goals were, she quickly responded, "I want to lose weight, be healthy, and have more stamina." She briefly mentioned how she had some cardiovascular issues, but she wasn't going to let any of that stop her. I remember putting her through the first workout, which consisted of endurance exercises, planks, modified push-ups, and squats to assess her stamina, strength, and coordination. After making her do jumping jacks and high knees, I was mortified when she had to stop and sit down. This was the first time this had ever happened during one of my sessions, and I felt like a complete failure as a trainer. Did I overestimate her abilities? Did I pick the wrong assessment exercises? Is she ever going to want to train with me again? All these thoughts were going through my head when I finally sat down next to Jenelle and said, "It's ok. This is your first time really working out. Don't be discouraged. You're doing phenomenal, your body just has to catch up with your ambition." She grinned at me and started to give me more details about her history with her heart. She said it has been something she has struggled with her whole life, and she gets frustrated that it disables her from doing certain things.

At that moment, the desire I have always had to hide my own medical challenges seemed to disappear. For the first time ever, I felt it was my responsibility to exemplify that anything is possible. I was nervous yet excited to tell Jenelle about my history and all of the obstacles I had to overcome to get to where I am today. To finally be able to open up to someone. She was so engrossed with what I had to say. She couldn't believe that even though I made fitness look so easy, I had to go through so much. I could see the instant spark of motivation in Jenelle's face once I told her my story. And her motivation made me feel a sense of strength mentally. One that I had never felt before. Although her session had long ended, I wanted her to finish what she started. I told her we were going to get up and try again. She was ready. She was determined. And she would become one of my next clients.

ROZ

I loved watching Kim train the older adults at the gym and thinking she had an amazing ability to help them with their fitness and also their overall quality of life. Although Jimi was about 60 when we first started training, and Adrianna from the spa was an older adult, I did not have too much experience training seniors. Adrianna and I only trained for a few months, and I didn't really count Jimi as being in his 60s because of his young, vibrant attitude.

It wasn't until I met Roz that I really understood what it was like to train this unique age group. I was instantly drawn to Roz. She's about my height, 5'2", has short curly brown hair, and an extremely friendly personality. As I introduced myself to her, I instantly felt a sense of comfort. From the start, she always reminded me of a young grandma figure. Hip yet caring. Unfiltered and honest, yet loving.

Our first session started off with the normal assessment questions I always made sure to ask. "What brings you to the gym?" "What are your health goals?" "Do you have any medical conditions or medications I need to be aware of?" Roz, having nothing particularly important to report, responded with, "No, no! None of that shit! I just want to feel fit and happy as I get older."

I always felt like I had to give the best possible session in a 30-minute period. I figured that if anyone is spending money for me to train them, they should get the most out of their buck. But if I wanted to gain clients of all different ages and fitness levels, my approach needed to change. I needed to slow down. And I learned this after training Roz for the first time. During Roz's assessment session, I made her start with running in place. Big mistake. She was instantly out of breath and totally flushed. Although this exercise may have been a bit ambitious, I was confused as to why her body reacted this way so quickly. It wasn't until halfway through the session when she told me, "Oh, by the way, my breathing is probably terrible because I used to smoke for more than half my life!" With this in mind, I felt a little more at ease knowing that my exercise choice wasn't all terrible. The second exercise I had her do was a squat. Roz would get extremely frustrated because her coordination was off, and her strength just wasn't there yet. I decided to start her off with a chair squat. I would make her sit up and down from the chair so that her body would start to get used to the movement. When I thought she was ready to do it without the chair, I told her I would slowly remove it as she was sitting. I guess she didn't understand the directions, or I didn't make myself clear enough, because she sat all the way down and hit her ass on the ground! Roz's first 30-minute session seemed like an eternity. And I was so embarrassed, as I'm sure she was. I thought I would never see her again. But she got right up, looked me in the eyes, started hysterically laughing, and said, "I don't care how long it takes me, I will squat! Sign me up, sweetie!"

I started Roz off on a once a week program. Each session was half an hour. Kim always taught me that the way to gain consistency with clients is to start them off slow. "You never want to sell them a package at first that is more than their car payment," she would tell me. "If they like you and see results, they will gradually start increasing. Remember, to be successful, you need to focus on quality. Quantity will come."

***

Kim was right. Quantity would come. But no matter how many clients I would gain from that point forward, I will always have my core four. Jimi has been busting my chops since day one and still continues to do so today. "You can never get rid of me. I'm like a hemorrhoid. I'll always be a pain in your ass!" Danielle went from wanting the perfect body for a wedding to training with me four to five times a week. Her shy and serious personality flourished into what is now a loud, outgoing, and confident one. She truly is one of my dearest friends and will always be a reminder of where I started and how I've grown. She's seen me frustrated. She's seen me get discouraged as a trainer if I felt like I wasn't giving my all. She's even been understanding when I would have to juggle my schoolwork with training. But she's never left. She always believes in me. Jenelle's white Adidas sneakers are not as bright as they once were, but her spirit is still as lively, and her squats are lower than she'd ever thought possible. My Saturdays have never been the same since Jenelle walked into my life. And I wouldn't want it any other way. As for Roz, she did indeed learn to squat. Her new-found stamina makes her seem as if she'd never smoked a day in her life. She has fallen in love with fitness so much that she went from doing half-hour sessions to hour sessions, at least three times a week! She will always be like a "gym-grandma" to me. She's been a listening ear and a constant supporter. My core four may have only been the beginning of my career. However, without the strength, resilience, and growth they've shown me, I may not have developed into who I am today.

Strength, Resilience, Growth

10 THE COMMUNITY CENTER

Transitioning Into My Own Personal Training Business

Whenever I introduce myself to someone, or meet a new client for the first time, everyone is always surprised at how young I am (just like Danielle was when she first met me). I've always considered myself an old soul. I've always appreciated old-school music, thanks to the guidance of my dad. I would rather go on the stair-master at the gym and listen to Queen or the Beatles, instead of the current music being played today. I like surrounding myself with older people because I feel as though I actually fit in. They understand me, and I respect them.

Besides my love for anything 1960s and onward, many people consider me older because of how quickly I advanced in my career so early on. After only a few months of being a trainer, I had many clients, including my core four, and many hours of training under my belt. I was now not only getting advice from Kim, but giving her pointers on how we can both maintain our success. But although life was great and the gym business was booming, I wasn't satisfied. This wasn't what I wanted my whole life to be. Even if it was just after three months! I didn't just want to work for a corporate gym, and I knew there were people out there who didn't want to train in one either.

It was July of 2017 when things started to change for me. My parents went to the Jersey shore the week of July 4th. This was the first time they had ever left me home alone. Nineteen years and I had never been left home alone for more than a few hours. Now I got a whole week to myself, and let me tell you, I was loving it. Since I had a lot of time, I really took the opportunity to think about my next move as a trainer.

One night, I went over to my friend's house after not seeing her or her family for months. I've known Betsy and her mother, Christine, ever since elementary school. Betsy and I would be the leads in school plays together, dreaming about what life would be like on Broadway. It is amazing to see where life has taken us, and now neither of us has a desire for Broadway anymore!

I sat down at their kitchen table, extremely excited to discuss what I've been up to. Christine has always treated me like a second daughter. She's been there for my parents and me when things were rough. She continues to always be supportive of my goals. I explained how great everything at the gym was going, but how I wanted more. I wanted to do my own thing. I wanted to train clients who weren't comfortable enough to go into the gym. I wanted to show people that fitness can be achieved anywhere.

After brainstorming a few ideas, Christine thought it may be a good idea to reach out to the local community center. Having some connections, she knew they may have some rooms available to rent. Without skipping a beat, I asked her, "Who do we call, and when can we do it?"

As my heart was racing and my palms were sweating, just like the day I got my training certificate, Christine made the phone call to her friend. The lady on the phone instantly put us in contact with the man who ran the community center and said he had actually been looking for a trainer to take up one of the rooms.

I left their house that night full of hope. I had a million thoughts running through my head about what my future could be if this worked out.

The next morning, I called my parents, who were still away, and told them I was headed to the community center to see if I could get a space for my training. They told me to be smart. That even though I wanted this badly, be mindful of pricing and don't get taken advantage of. But I knew that wouldn't be a problem. My parents taught me the value of money since I was very young. With any dollar I ever got, whether it be birthday money, a graduation gift, or even a reward from the tooth fairy, I was always expected to save half. So I knew that I was going to fight for a fair deal. I walked into the bright building feeling a little uneasy. I was nervous about meeting the man because I had never handled a situation like this without my parents. But when I walked in, a middle-aged Italian man with big brown eyes looked at me, held out his hand, and said, "Hi, you must be Gigante. I'm Johnny."

A Man Named Johnny

There are some people you meet in life that you click with instantly. The day I shook Johnny's hand was the start of a relationship I will never forget. Johnny was drawn to my drive for health and fitness. He liked that a girl as young as me had the guts to walk right into his office and negotiate with him. Without thinking twice, he offered me a small little space conducive enough for training clients. I was thrilled but knew I should wait for mom and dad before making a final decision.

A few days later, when my parents came home, we all went to meet up with Johnny. My parents fell in love with him just as he had grown a quick liking to them. They felt that the community center was a good start for what I wanted to do. And Johnny promised, "Sophia is in good hands here. She's part of the family now." So, the papers were signed, the keys were handed over, and I was ready for this next new chapter.

The community center became like a second home. I was still working at the gym, but now I was focusing on building up my own clientele. I started training some clients, like Jimi and Danielle, privately. I even started gaining new ones as word started going around about me. Johnny always helped me advertise my business. He made it a point to let me know about any events that were going on in the community. He would get me involved in the local fireworks show, or the fairs. He would let me put my business cards all over the community center and told everyone he knew about me. As time went on, Johnny really did become like family to me. He would make sure I always had everything I needed in my little training room. He would call or text me periodically to see how I was doing if he hadn't seen me in a while. He would even stay at work late if I was there sometimes just so that I wouldn't be leaving alone.

Johnny would laugh and make fun of my anxious habits. I remember one time I locked myself out of my training room and was freaking out because I was going to be late for my night class at school. Frantically, I called Johnny and was in tears, trying to apologize for making such a stupid mistake. All he had said was, "Gigante, calm down. It's not the end of the world. You need to learn how to relax when things like this happen." And he was right. But this wasn't going to be the first time he would see this anxious side of me.

Johnny and I spent a lot of time together. I would talk to him when I was stressed out about things, or when I just needed some good advice. He would always say something like, "Come on Gigante. We have to find you a nice man. You've got your hobby, you got your business, but now you need to be treated to a nice date." He always made me smile.

I started to realize who I truly was as a trainer during my time at the community center. I was training there almost every day, and getting to work with new clients. During this time, I also began helping those with special needs. Given my work at the gym and the community center, word had gotten around that I have incredible patience and would be a great fit for anyone needing some extra help. I started helping those with autism, epilepsy, and even stroke victims. But at that time, I didn't realize how important this population would be for my career.

Within a year at the community center, I created a business. I spent hours training people and setting up group fitness classes for anyone in Westchester interested in joining. I even got certified as a Sports Nutrition Specialist because I loved nutrition and wanted it to be a part of my services. I will never forget the smile Johnny always gave me as he watched me do what I love. He believed in me. He admired me. And no matter what, he would always protect me.

The Special Needs Population

By the time I reached the two-year mark at the community center, I was extremely busy with clients. At this point, I got even more serious about training those with special needs. This population was becoming extremely important to me. I found myself starting to share my childhood experiences with them because they understood better than anyone. I also felt it was my responsibility to exemplify how anything is achievable if you put your mind to it. I began training many autistic children and adults. I loved seeing how health and fitness made daily life tasks easier for them. I even helped many of them change their nutrition habits. They loved learning about healthy foods and how it would benefit their bodies. I started training a man who was left paralyzed from a stroke but promised him that with hard work and determination, we would get his life back. And that's exactly what we did. After just a few months of training with me, the man started gaining strength back and was able to walk straight and do push-ups. I found myself teaching him exercises that I used to do during physical therapy. I finally started realizing all of the hard work Myrielle did to help me get stronger. These movements that I once dreaded, such as walking backward or balancing on one foot, were now part of my plan to help my client. I have never felt so happy and accomplished to see him succeed. He continues to work hard during each session we have and sees improvement each time.

I started helping clients who suffer from anxiety. I felt a deep sense of compassion for these individuals since I was beginning to struggle more with anxiety as well. The more I helped people with special needs, the more I became in touch with my own feelings. This forced me to address things I had been shying away from. I enjoyed sharing my story with others, but something was happening. All of these buried feelings left me overwhelmed with PTSD and anxiety. I started remembering those childhood experiences I once promised myself I would forget. I loved helping others but found myself crying in my car after long days, reminiscing about all those doctor's appointments, seizures, and long physical therapy sessions. I was grateful for my current success, but at the same time, trying to deal with past emotions. However, this did not stop me from helping others. If anything, it made my work feel more worthwhile. My early life challenges helped me empathize with my clients and gave me special insight into what they were going through.

Johnny Helped Me Find Myself

It was July of 2019. Mom and dad had left for their yearly trip to the Jersey Shore, and I was occupied with all of my clients. I got a text message from Johnny saying he wanted to talk to me as soon as possible. My anxiety sky-rocketed as I drove myself to see him. I felt just as uneasy walking in to see him as I did when we first met. When I walked into his office, he looked me in the eyes and said, "Gigante, I got some bad news. Things have changed around here, and only a few people on the board are allowed to have a key to the center. And you're not one of them." My heart sank. Tears started to roll down my face. "You can still use your training room. But you just can't have access unless I am here." I was angry. I was sad. I felt like everything I worked for was falling apart. I started to yell and show Johnny a whole different side of myself. A side I didn't even know existed. This anger was so out of character for me. "How could this happen? How could I still train here with those rules? I work on my own schedule, and my clients rely on their specific times." Despite my rudeness, Johnny looked at me with his big smile and said, "Gigante. I told you. You are family. I will make this work."

Johnny did make it work. He worked around my schedule. He came to the community center on weekends just so I could train my clients. He even got other employees on the board to come in and open the doors for me if he wasn't available. He did everything for me. But I knew this wouldn't last. And Johnny knew too.

One day as I was finishing up my sessions, Johnny came to talk to me. "Gigante. What are you still doing here? I mean, I love you, and I love seeing you train here, but you're better than this." I told him I had been looking around for new spaces to train out of and was trying to figure out my next move. "Well, look harder."

"Oh, and by the way, who are you?"

I looked at him confused and said, "I'm Sophia?"

"We can't just keep referring to you as Sophia, the trainer. You need a name for your business. For who you are."

"Well, I don't know what else to call myself."

"Well, what are your initials?" He said with his iconic smirk.

"SRG."

"Good, now go out there, and make them stand for something."

And that's exactly what I did.

Strength, Resilience, Growth

11 SRG FITNESS

Moving on From the Community Center

My dad always told me that when you love what you do, you never work a day in your life. He's right. I love what I do. I also believe that there is nothing better in life than living out your passion. And I have been lucky enough to find my passion at a young age. I never dread waking up early or staying up late to help my clients achieve their goals. Despite how small my training space was in the community center, I never complained. In my heart, I knew it was only the beginning. I knew it was the start of the path that I was meant to be on. To do what I was meant to do. But if I wanted to grow physically, mentally, and as a health professional, it was time to move on from what I was comfortable with. It was time to create SRG FITNESS.

Some may think they are biased, but if you ask my parents, they will tell you I was always destined to do something incredible in this world. I was born with such hardships and managed to work through each and every one of them. My parents have always believed there was a reason for that. I remember thinking this as I sat down the night after talking to Johnny. I thought the idea of my initials for a business name would be cool. I thought it would be even better if they stood for something that I believed in. Something that I could preach to those around me. Strength, resilience, and growth seemed to fit perfectly. It really portrayed everything I have overcome, and everything I aim to achieve.

I spent the next few weeks trying to find the perfect studio location. I did everything on my own. I made numerous phone calls, spent hours traveling through local towns to look at spaces, and negotiated with property owners. I knew what I wanted. And I was determined to get it. I wanted a nice-sized studio. One that would be conducive enough for one-on-one training and nutrition counseling. But most importantly, one that I can make my own. After an entire summer of searching, I finally landed upon my studio in Yonkers, New York, which was ironic, since Yonkers is where my journey as a personal trainer began. Just like Johnny, the property owners saw the potential in me. They were impressed with my drive and ambition at only 21-years-old. They were more than happy to hand me over my new key. Everything was falling into place.

My parents were happy with my decision. After a couple of years at the community center, they felt this was the perfect next step for my career. Once I finalized everything with the new studio, it was time to make it my own. My parents helped me bring my vision to life. Instead of hiring a painter, or a professional flooring company to get the work done, we did everything on our own. That's the amazing thing about my parents. They have always supported my goals. They will do anything to help turn my dreams into reality.

I planned to open the studio in October of 2019. This gave us only two months to get things in order. My mom helped paint my bright rose gold walls to match my new logo for SRG FITNESS. My dad put down a whole gym floor so that clients would have a comfortable ground to exercise on. I bought all the equipment needed to turn my new space into the best workout studio. We put flyers all around Westchester County. We did everything together. We didn't need anyone else's help. If we got through everything else in life together, putting a studio in order was a piece of cake. And one that was well worth the labor!

Bringing Clients Into SRG FITNESS

I'll never forget the grand opening of my studio. October 6, 2019. I was so excited as I got ready that morning. I actually spent time putting makeup on (something I never do) and made sure my SRG FITNESS attire was perfect. My mom, dad, and I walked in that day, ready to prepare everything for everyone coming to view it. We set out tables full of SRG FITNESS shirts, business cards, and other marketing materials. I had sign-up sheets ready for anyone wanting to book sessions with me. I felt like I was on top of the world. For the first time, I truly felt like I found my place. I was no longer the little girl struggling to catch up with her friends because she couldn't walk straight. I was no longer the outcast in high school because I wasn't into the party scene. Instead, I was SRG. The confident, intelligent, kickass health professional, opening her own business.

My eyes lit up every time I saw people come in to see my new space. So many of my clients throughout the past few years, as well as some family and friends, came to see what SRG FITNESS was all about. And everyone loved it. I had new-comers signing up for sessions, and old clients come to support me and tell others how much they love working with me. Out of all those who came that day, I will always remember the look on Jimi, Danielle, Jenelle, and Roz's faces. They were so proud of me. I loved listening to them tell everyone how they were my first clients and how I changed their lives. They have always said that the gym was only the beginning for me. It turns out they were right. My grand opening wouldn't have been complete without them. Because although they are clients, they have become family.

That day was only the beginning of how much my business would grow within the next few months. I got so busy training clients, holding nutrition seminars, and advertising my business, that college was really hard to manage. I never went back to Manhattan College that year because I wasn't happy there, and I really didn't have the time. But academics have always been important to me, and my parents were not going to let me give up school completely. So, I found a way to earn my degree while running SRG FITNESS. I decided to finish my degree online through Arizona State University. Not only would I complete my degree in nutrition, but I would also become a certified health coach for life once I take all the necessary classes. It was a perfect fit. Between online classes and my training career, the only thing left to do is be open to any next steps life has in store for me.

Navigating Personal Challenges

One of the first movies my dad ever had me watch as a little girl was Rocky. He always wanted me to know that no matter what life throws at me, anything is possible. A quote that has always stuck with me from the movie was, "It ain't how hard you hit... It's how hard you can get hit and keep moving forward. It's about how much you can take and keep moving forward!" So much so that I have it tattooed on my ankle.

I wish I could say that everything was easy when starting a business and focusing on a specific way of life. But unfortunately, although this was such a positive time for me, it also came with some challenges. One of the hardest things I've ever had to deal with was being a health professional in an Italian family. As I got serious in my career, I started receiving negative comments and uncertain looks from my extended family, who I thought would be excited about my new path. The judgments were endless. At every family event, without fail, I would get asked about why I don't eat certain foods or how small my waist is. I would get stares if I chose to eat chicken and vegetables. My family would make comments about how I work out every day. They would ask questions like, "Oh, so you're going to work as a trainer for your career?" And when I would show off any of my exercise routines, I always had to hear, "You are going to get hurt lifting that weight. You should stop."

In addition to expressing negativity about my career path, my family members also felt confused about my new college choice. They were concerned about how I was getting a degree without being in a classroom, and what exactly this degree would do for my future. I swallowed a big lump in my throat to hold back the anger when having to defend all of my life decisions. I felt like that little girl again who always had to explain herself to people that couldn't seem to understand. I felt discouraged and hurt. I never understood why, after years of struggling both physically and mentally, my family members couldn't see how positive this transition was for me.

I would constantly talk to my mom about my feelings. Although she understood my discouragement, she reminded me that my family didn't know the extent of my struggles and what I've overcome. They knew about all my conditions, they knew I had to take precautions, but they never saw the full picture. My parents made it a point to never victimize me or what the three of us were going through. They never complained about the numerous doctor's appointments or the long hours of physical therapy. They showed up at every family event as if we were living a normal life. And that is what my family saw.

Through this experience, I've learned the importance of never judging someone from the outside. Before questioning anyone's motivation for doing something, it is important to remember that everyone has a story. I am grateful to be able to tell mine. It has brought me closer to my own feelings, as well as my loved ones around me.

12 JUST THE BEGINNING

Some of the most common things I hear from people about working out is, "I hate going to the gym. I feel like everyone is looking at me. I feel ashamed. I don't know what to do when I am there." Well, I have news for everyone. The best thing about physical fitness is that it is a personal sport. You are only competing against yourself. You are hitting new goals each time you step into a gym or any type of fitness center. No one at the gym cares about anyone else but themselves. So walk in there, and be proud. Be ready to crush your own goals.

If the gym isn't for you, that doesn't mean exercise is out of the question. Fitness is not one size fits all. It can be tailored to anyone based on goals, personal preferences, and strengths and weaknesses. You can exercise at home, outside, or anywhere you feel comfortable. Make this an enjoyable experience and an essential part of daily life. Don't ever be intimated to strengthen your body.

Just like fitness, nutrition varies for the individual. My goal is to help people figure out the best way to incorporate proper nutrients into their life. When working with me, you will never hear the word "Diet." If you are looking for a quick fix, you have come to the wrong person. Instead, I will work with you to make sure that you are eating nutritious foods in an enjoyable way. Nutrition and fitness are meant to be sustainable. They are the most powerful medicine.

After everything I've overcome, I feel my mission in life is to show others that anything is possible. The worst experience for me was feeling like I was not in control of my body. It is the most frightening thing when you are restricted by the unknown. This is why I am committed to empowering others to take charge of their perceived limitations. To encourage them to stop making excuses for bad choices. To choose good health overall. To put their mind, soul, and body before anything else. I've met some extraordinary people who have dealt with setbacks. I have seen them work hard to fight the odds. If we all can work through these difficult challenges, the easiest thing left to do is treat our bodies with good health. What you do today will be the foundation of your tomorrow.

Hydrocephalus will always be a part of me. Hypotonia will always make me work harder to achieve physical milestones. Seizures will always be an uncomfortable memory. But none of them will ever define me. I am who I am because of them, but I am not them. I am better than them. I am Strength. I am Resilience. I am Growth.

WE DID IT, LITTLE SOPH!

Strength, Resilience, Growth

ABOUT THE AUTHOR

Sophia Rose Gigante is an NCSF Certified Personal Trainer and NASM Certified Sports Nutrition Specialist. At just 22 years old, while finishing her degree in Health Coaching and Nutrition, Sophia has created her own business, SRG FITNESS. SRG FITNESS is a personal training and nutrition counseling wellness studio located in Westchester, New York. Sophia welcomes everyone with open arms. She builds training programs and nutrition plans that are specifically tailored to each individual. And brings all aspects of health and wellness into her clients' lives via in-person sessions and worldwide virtual trainings.

Sophia gives more than just sets and reps at SRG FITNESS. She understands each client's needs and reflects upon her personal experiences to ensure that each client feels in control of their bodies. At SRG FITNESS, Sophia also specializes in helping clients with special needs. She has worked with stroke victims, as well as clients with Autism, anxiety disorders, Scoliosis, and Epilepsy. She believes that physical fitness and proper nutrition can be the best medicine for clients with special needs.

SRG FITNESS is an all-inclusive health and wellness experience. Sophia believes that everyone is entitled to health and wellness. She wants everyone, especially the "underdogs," to always feel strength, resilience, and growth when walking into SRG FITNESS.

Sophia has been featured on News 12, and in publications such as, The Hydrocephalus Association Blog, Kivo Daily, Y Not You Media Blog, and The Eastchester Review, to name a few.

Learn more at:
sophiagigante.com
Instagram: srg.fit
Facebook: SRG FITNESS
LinkedIn: Sophia Gigante

Strength, Resilience, Growth

TESTIMONIALS

"It was April 29, 2018. The day of my stroke and my rebirth. I am not one to just sit and wait for things to happen. So, after eight weeks of therapy, I decided that I needed a personal trainer. On July 4, 2018, I met Sophia Rose Gigante. From that very first meeting, I knew we were the perfect match. She was very patient. She knew just how to push me without going overboard. As time passed, she became more than my trainer and "therapist." She became my friend. I can talk about Sophia for hours to anyone who would listen. It is now two years later, and I still look forward to our time together. I don't know where I would be on my current journey without her. I am and will forever be her HYPE man."

– Robert Noel

"SRG FITNESS has greatly helped me improve my lifestyle. I am in better shape and I'm eating much healthier than I was before. Sophia is a very talented trainer who's great at knowing your limits but also pushing you to do your best."

— Ethan Krauss

"I have had weight issues since I was 10 years old. I was an overweight kid who grew up self-conscious and scared of food, thinking that I would gain back the weight I had lost at any time due to poor self-control and never be satisfied with what I saw in the mirror. This all changed once I started at SRG FITNESS. What began as a quick three months to get my body right for a wedding turned into a lifetime of better choices, better eating habits, and a stronger sense of self-control. With a meal plan tailored specifically for my body and four training sessions a week, Sophia has made me feel empowered when I eat and confident whenever I look in the mirror. I have learned that when you understand the science behind food and push yourself to exercise consistently, your self-esteem flourishes, and food no longer seems like an addiction you can't control. Thank you, Sophia, for not only getting my body right but for literally transforming my life."

– Danielle Green

"When I first met Sophia, I didn't think she would become a part of my life the way she has. Not only has she helped me lose weight, but she has guided me towards a healthier lifestyle. Sophia has even taken me food shopping multiple times to make sure that I am not eating any more crap! She has changed my life for the better."

– Jimi M.

"It was a 'perfect storm' so to speak. I was 65 years old, overweight, out of shape, an ex-smoker, and I never worked out or belonged to a gym. Then one day, I met Sophia. This was over three years ago. Sophia became a true trainer, a teacher, a motivator. She had such insight and empathy for someone her age and a powerful spirit and drive. She quickly became like a daughter to me (my fifth daughter, since I already had four). I needed to be taught to exercise. I needed to learn not to injure myself and maintain a healthy exercise plan. Sophia was just so good at keeping me going and seeing what I was capable of. It's so true that if you don't move every day, it becomes more painful when you do. I have overcome that with the help and encouragement of Sophia. I tell my daughters, "You can thank Sophia that I haven't broken my hip yet. I am healthy, stronger than ever, and confident that I can do more than I can't." Sophia brought me into her family and I brought her into mine. My daughters appreciate that I am aging strong. Sophia is a role model for all of us. No matter how old you are, no matter what shape you are in, and no matter what you can and cannot do, she will reach in and find it and she did."

– Roz Coco Canon

"   "There are times when the depths of darkness envelop all folds of life. All thoughts coated in self-pity. There's an overwhelming sentiment that overtakes you; you awaken with it – despair. This emotion, many times, is equally paired with doubt and resentment. Of what you may ask, resentment of the longing for that one emotion we all seek, happiness. In our modern day, it seems so elusive, and it would appear that every effort to gain true joy is misguided and ultimately worthless. Just a mere three years ago, these were the feelings that inhabited me. At this time, I met an amazing human being who would impart major change in my life. That person is Sophia Rose Gigante.

I'd been overeating, self-indulging in every high caloric food and beverage my eyes set upon. Now mind you, I'd already been a member of the gym for a few years, but self-admittedly, I hadn't put any "real work" in. My exercise regimen, if you want to call it that, consisted of a few days a month, and nothing intense at that. For me, the weight section was a forbidden land I dare not enter without a proper travel guide.

It was around this time that I was introduced to Sophia. Something in me, a little voice, said, "Jenelle, go for it. What do you have to lose?" And so I did. That will hold to be one of the best decisions of my life. From the onset of my initial training meeting, I knew Sophia would not only become my trainer, but also a friend. Upon meeting her, I had a feeling that this training thing was not only unchartered territory for me, but also for her. You see, I was one of her first clients. Surprisingly though, Sophia was a natural. Without much effort, she had figured me out, and our training schedule ensued. Our workouts were like a sitcom. We had so much to talk about. However, our conversations, my comedic timing, and her workout instruction, still made for an effective workout. Our chemistry just flowed, so natural that you knew our partnership was meant to be. All that aside, I won't be selfish because that is just who Sophia is.

In the last few years, I've had the pleasure of attending events that Sophia has hosted, from nutritional courses to bootcamps and have had the pleasure of meeting other clients, and family and friends. They all share the same sentiments, "Sophia is one of a kind." "Her setbacks were her stepping stones." "She never gives up!" I can go on and on, but the thing is, they are all true! Sophia not only trains, but digs deep to get to know her clients, their lives and quirks, and all the trimmings that make a person whole. I can't say if she knew it at the onset of our meeting, but I did; I would stick with the training and more importantly, stick with Sophia.

Her nature, ever so compassionate but stern, kept me on a focused path of elevation, physically and more. Every workout started with a question, "How are you Jenelle? How's your mom and family?" In the chaos of this world, it feels good to know you are cared for. Sophia cares. She works the mind, body, and soul. I've risen to levels in life that I can honestly say is in part due to the training and friendship we share. This new Jenelle lives life on purpose!

Sophia, I remember years ago, when I planted the seed and said, "You have a story that needs to be told, write a book." Then, it was just an idea, but thankfully you latched on to it, and now to see it come to fruition makes me smile deep from the inside. This is just the beginning for you. Your story will continue to unfold, and I'm grateful to see you rise into your next chapter of greatness."

– Jenelle Brown

NOTES

Strength, Resilience, Growth

Strength, Resilience, Growth

Strength, Resilience, Growth

Strength, Resilience, Growth

Made in the USA
Middletown, DE
10 September 2020

19016117R00066